OBEDIENCE OVER PERFECTION

OBEDIENCE OVER PERFECTION

TEMEKA
THOMPSON

Marriage
Takeover®
Publishing
Maryland, USA
2025

Published by Marriage Takeover® Publishing
An imprint of Marriage Takeover®
Waldorf, Maryland, USA

Editorial Services Provided By:
Developmental Editor: Byrd's World Publishing

Hardcover: 978-1-7372872-2-3
Softcover: 978-1-7372872-1-6
Audiobook: 978-1-7372872-3-0

Cover design by L3 Design
Interior design by Jesamae A.Omallao
Printed in the United States of America

Credits

Bengtson, M. (2017, August 23). DrMichelleBengtson.com. https://drmichellebengtson.com/role-forgiveness-healing-brain-heart/

Scripture quotations are taken from YouVersion. (n.d.). Bible. New Living Translation, The Passion Translation, Life.Church. Retrieved September 13, 2025, from https://www.bible.com. All rights reserved.

 First Edition. Printed in the USA.

TABLE OF CONTENTS

DEDICATION

This book is dedicated to all the great giants in my life that have transitioned. Thank you for paving the way for me to be who I am today. Your legacy lives on.

I love you all and miss you so much.

Author's Note

This is my love letter to every woman, every teenage girl, every little girl who never thought she was good enough, pretty enough, smart enough, sexy enough, wise enough, or had enough to pursue purpose. For the woman who felt she didn't have a voice. For the woman whose voice was taken. For the woman who thought she never had enough value to offer the world. This is my life poured out for you, and I invite you, sis, to pursue purpose again and again until you're sitting in the life you dreamed of, the life God always had set apart just for you.

Preface

Like many women, I mastered the art of becoming what everyone else needed, showing up strong, putting on a smile, performing for applause while silently suffocating behind closed doors. I was the helper. The wife. The mom. The fixer. The singer. The one who always made a way for someone. The show-up-for-everybody-but-me woman. And for a long time, I thought that was enough. That maybe purpose was just wrapped up in service without self-discovery. But something in my soul started whispering: There's more.

This book is born from that whisper.

It's for the woman who's not sure if she has a gift. It's for the woman who can't determine what her gifts are because they're buried beneath shame and guilt. For the woman who feels like her dreams are buried underneath her duties so she believes she has to perform for everything. For the woman who's not sure she even matters. For the woman who silently wonders if she missed her moment. For the high-achiever who secretly feels stuck. For the faith-filled woman who shows up for church but struggles to show up for herself.

For the woman who hasn't yet had the capacity to dream bigger. And for the woman leading an empire sitting in a corner office, yet still questioning her worth.

This is for you, sis.

Let me be clear: this is not a book about how to "hustle harder" or "manifest" your way into a six-figure purpose. This is about pursuing purpose with intentional obedience, even when it costs you comfort. It's about healing the wounds that sabotage your next. It's about confronting the lies you've believed, the trauma you've normalized, and the version of you that's been surviving but not thriving.

And I want to be very clear, this ain't your grandmother's religion. I've broken all the church rules to make room for you at the table. This is a journey of the living word.

In these pages, I'll tell you my truth unfiltered. I'll take you back to moments I questioned my calling, doubted my worth, and almost gave up on my own life. But I'll also show you what happened when I finally surrendered to those moments, really trusting God and allowing Him to carry me. When I decided that obedience would be my strategy. When I learned that healing wasn't just personal, it is positional. That I had to be made whole not just for me, but for the assignment attached to my name.

Every chapter is a mirror and a map:

- A mirror to help you confront who you've become while surviving.
- A map to guide you toward who you were always created to be and to remind you that you no longer have to remain in survival mode.

Each chapter will offer a My Life Poured Out moment offering a reflective quote, affirmations, and a Midwife Moment. The Midwife moments are transformational exercises to help you push, breathe and birth something from within.

This journey will challenge you, but it will also change you. There will be journal moments, “ouch, that hit me” moments, and freedom filled moments that shake the dust off of your dreams.

I’m not here to give you formulas. I’m here to walk with you through your birthing season.

Whether you’re in a corporate boardroom, behind a register, leading in church, raising babies, or building empires. Purpose isn’t just possible, it’s assigned to you.

And sis, there’s a nation waiting on your yes.

Intro

> "You don't need every answer to begin, you just need enough faith to say yes and take the first step."
>
> \- Temeka Thompson

Just start it, damn it.

That's literally what I told myself to get in motion to write this book.

I sat in front of a blank screen, frustrated. Paralyzed. Overthinking every sentence before I ever typed a single word. I had every excuse rehearsed:

"What if it's not the right time?"
"What if nobody reads it?"
"What if they think I'm not qualified?"
"What if they don't like it?"
"What if it doesn't sell?"

The truth is, I was just scared.

Scared that putting this on paper meant I couldn't hide anymore. Scared that obedience would cost me the version of myself I had worked so hard to protect. Scared that I had to be responsible for a version of myself I wasn't even sure I understood.

And then I heard it get louder and louder like an aggravating pesky mosquito you know is flying around in your car, but you can't find it. You know it's near because it keeps biting you, yep, that type of aggravation... "Just start it, damn it."

Yes, I talk to myself like that. Because sometimes you need to shock your fear out of the driver's seat and take the wheel with trembling hands and a steady heart, so you can move.

Here's the truth I had to confront:
"*Purpose doesn't wait on perfect conditions.*"

It doesn't care if your ducks are in a row. And it doesn't need your confidence to match your calling. Purpose moves on obedience. And obedience? It often feels inconvenient, uncomfortable, and uncertain. Unfortunately, obedience is never optional when you're chosen.

Let me ask you something, how long have you been sitting on the thing God told you to do?

The blog.
The business.
The relationship.
The boundary.
The book.
The ministry.
The bold conversation.
The becoming.

How long have you been gathering information, watching webinars, attending conferences, watching everybody else move, but still not activating what God placed in you?

There comes a point where delay isn't wisdom, it's disobedience dressed up in busyness and fear. Yes I said it, I'll say it again for the people in the back. It's clear disobedience dressed up as busyness and fear. And for me? This book had been sitting in delay long enough.

I mean seriously. I've been writing short stories and novels since I was a kid. I never knew it then, I just always thought I had a great imagination. Because we moved so much I have no idea where all the stories landed. It seemed like every two years we were de-cluttering, packing up and moving so I'm sure those pages have disintegrated deep beneath the earth's surface in someone's landfill. But if those grounds could talk, baby, the stories they would tell.

Then I was supposed to write a book after surviving the 9/11 attacks on the Pentagon and didn't think I had enough or knew enough to author a book. Then God actually showed me I was an author and told me to again write my first book before I released my first gospel album in 2006. Then again, He nudged me in 2020 during the Pandemic when I had nothing but time. And then again in 2021 when my husband and I
released our first book together. And what I told myself and God was, "See God, I wrote the book. I was obedient." Knowing good and well, I didn't give God my full yes. Now I know I'm not alone in this. We play around with instructions, we play around with what we thought God said, we play around with how we're supposed to do the thing all because in the back of our minds, we don't believe He's called the right one. We don't believe we're capable of doing the very thing God has called us to do. We don't feel adequate or worthy so we posture ourselves in disobedience.

This Isn't About a Book—It's About Permission

Saying "yes" to writing this book wasn't about ink and paper. It wasn't about book sales and a book tour. And it wasn't about waiting on someone to give me permission to go. It was about finally giving myself permission to own my story, to be seen, to believe God didn't call me accidentally. It was about giving myself permission to be authentically me. It was about giving myself permission to be judged by others and being okay with their judgment, understanding it doesn't define me.

Yes I still use curse words.

It's about giving myself permission to be judged by others who don't know or understand my relationship with God. I am a worshiper at heart and I'm not perfect. I had to give myself permission to be okay with letting the world see I'm not perfect and judge me. I had to give myself permission to know I'm not for everybody, but there's a nation of women and girls waiting on my **yes**. Not my perfect yes. But my fully surrendered and obedient yes.

I had to get to that point in my life where I loved me enough. Not the conceited arrogant loving me. Not the *me against the world loving me*. Not the *be perfect so everybody can love me*, me. But the seeing *all of my flaws and loving them as much as I love my dimples, me.* That gentle loving me. And she's actually pretty damn AMAZING.

Sweet wine, red or white are my friends (at least at the writing of this book). I had to give myself permission to be judged by others who don't understand that I love God, honor Him, worship Him and adore Him and He loves me too and I still drink wine. And to date, He hasn't convicted me or told me to put it down. These are my vices that often bring division in the Body of Christ and I had to be okay with being a woman of God in leadership and being judged.

I'm super silly. I mean stupid silly. But I've had to be the responsible one all of my life. The responsible one earned promotions. The responsible one earned a great salary. The person most people looked to. I made responsibility my cape, my badge of honor. So I tucked away the silly part of me for only those who earned the right to get close enough to experience the softer version of me. So I've had to learn to love every single aspect of me and be okay with the me I've grown to love and be judged. And that's not easy because people are brutal and this "cancel culture" is fierce. And let's not talk about the judgment and hypocrisy from the church, it'll make you walk away from God if you don't really have a true relationship with Him.

Let me be very clear, this book isn't just about me having something to say; it's that *you do too*. And I had to push past my fears so I could unlock yours.

Starting this book was liberating. It was me telling shame to shut up. It was me firing fear. It was me walking barefoot across the shards of my old self so I could bleed into something beautiful, not just for me, but for you to see it's possible for you as well.

And let me tell you—*bleeding publicly* ain't cute.

Obedience is never about aesthetics.

It's about assignment.

Now before I truly bleed publicly let me set the stage for you so you know I really do love my family.

My mother was absolutely amazing. She's the real MVP. She was breathtakingly beautiful. Her laugh could heal your soul, and her smile lit up every room she stepped into with her pecan-tan skin. She had deep dimples, like someone had gently carved joy right into her cheeks, and yes, that's exactly where I get mine from. Her charisma carried weight. When she entered a room, the atmosphere shifted. And she was fine...the kind of fine that made people stop mid-sentence. She had a classic Coca-Cola, hourglass figure that turned heads everywhere we went. My sister and I would walk right behind her at the grocery store to block other men's view of her butt — our small, funny attempt at protecting what we knew was radiant. She dressed with such class, turning the simplest outfits into statements. Tights and jogging pants became fashion when she paired them with pumps and a cute belt. She was wearing blazers with shorts before it was even a thing back in the '80s and '90s. Image mattered to her, not out of vanity but pride. She wouldn't step out looking undone and neither could her girls. Her hair flowed with her laughter and her stride, and baby, that woman could cut some hair. Doing hair was her sanctuary. She was known for her flawless cuts and became the family's resident stylist, transforming heads and hearts in her chair.

She was the hardest working single mother I've ever known. She juggled two to three jobs at a time, nursing school in the mornings, doing hair at the salon by day, and working nights at the hospital. On weekends or between shifts, she still found time to do family and friends' hair. She and my great-grandmother taught me what work ethic truly meant. I was a latchkey kid who learned early how to cook grits, eggs, hot dogs, and waffles for my sister and me while Mama worked and went to school. We had code rules for opening the door, had to decipher Morris code calls before caller ID existed, and an unspoken understanding that she was doing what she had to do to take care of us. She never complained, but I could see the weariness in her eyes. Still, she showed up, always. The older I get, the more I recognize her in me, from the way I raise my children and handle life's weight to the small, simple joys she loved. She adored fresh flowers and would buy roses, trim the leaves, and place them on the kitchen island just to watch them bloom. I never understood it back then, but guess who does that now? LOL—it's my therapy, too. She always smelled divine, a true Victoria's Secret lady. She'd even put on perfume before bed. I never got that as a teenager either, but now? I understand. When you love yourself, you do things that make you feel good, not for anyone else, but for you.

And she was wise. She knew which battles were worth fighting and which weren't. She had emotional intelligence long before we had a name for it. She loved people deeply and spoke with intention, everything she said came straight from the heart. If you didn't like her, honestly, it was probably jealousy. Her empathy was unmatched, her advice balanced and free of judgment—except when it came to disciplining her kids. Then it was all business—LOL! I wasn't the perfect child, and between my sister and me, I was definitely the one who gave her a run for her money. I'll never forget one day in high school when I got to leave early after finals. Carolyn came home unexpectedly, saw me sitting in the living room, and said, "What the hell are you doing home?" Before I could even answer, she flew across the room and had me pinned up against the wall by my throat! She thought I was skipping school and nearly snatched the breath out of me. When my feet finally hit the carpet and I showed her my notes from school, she gathered herself, and went on about her business, I guess she needed to calm down—LOL! That moment reminds me of her fierce love. She wasn't just enforcing the rules; she was protecting my future.

And the strength didn't start with my mother, it's the Ford legacy. The wisdom in our family runs deep. They gave tough love, but it was always balanced with the kind of wisdom that prepared you for a world that doesn't always love you back. Our family has this saying, "Built Ford Tough." I know Ford might've coined it first, but it truly defines our heritage. We come from a line of overcomers, people who faced hardship with grit, grace, and a faith that refused to bend.

What I love most about our family is that everybody is welcome. Regardless of color, or circumstance, your background, your beliefs, your status, your sexual orientation—none of it mattered. You were accepted and loved right where you were. That kind of open-armed love still speaks through my life today. We were taught to judge people not by the shade of their skin but by the fruit of their character. And that legacy still lives on, generations later.

My great-grandmother (affectionately known as "Grandma") was THE ultimate trailblazer. She was so wise. She taught me so much about life. Let me just say the women in my family are solid. Shelling peas, shucking corn, gathering the sugarcane and hanging clothes on the clothesline in the Florida hot sun were some of my favorite childhood memories. As we worked she would talk and the stories she would tell. The miles she walked and things she overcame.

Acquiring acres of land as a woman of color so her family would have a place to stay, being a business woman selling crops and pecans and the fruits of her labor to provide for her family and then creating a trust to protect it. Every time I go back home to visit, I stand on our family compound with pride because she literally built it from the ground up. She had all of these wise sayings and parables.

She would tell me often, "for every dollar you get, save you a quarter." Grandma was the real (greatest of all time) G.O.A.T.

Now my grandmother (affectionately known as "Gramps") was fierce, and I believe with everything in me that fussing was her love language. I remember her drinking ice coffee all day and fussing. She talked to herself a lot, I think that's where I get it from. Gramps was always there. I never went hungry and she always made room for us. Now every family member can't make it in the book, but I love each and every one of them, they really are amazing. At the time of writing this book (2024), quite a few gained their wings over the last year (my Gramps included). A rich legacy of wealth, wisdom, hard work, laughter, faith, love and being authentic will live on for generations.

My father is genius smart. He has the ability to remember things, I really believe he has photographic memory. He has this magical ability to retain information, process it in a matter of seconds, and teach it in a way anybody could understand it. There is nothing my father can't learn or figure out. And he's not bad looking either, a little silver fox. He always dressed so sharp, I can see how he and my mother were attracted to each other. I've never seen my dad in sweats; he typically wears a freshly crisp hard starch ironed shirt and slacks with really nice shoes. He's been in the automobile industry as long as I can remember, starting in sales and then becoming an owner-operator of his 18-wheel truck until he retired. He's always had big dreams, great desires, and not enough people close enough to help him bring everything into existence. He was so busy helping everyone else push their business and left his on the back burner. He has some amazing testimonies and prophecies over his life the world needs to hear. Back in the 1970s, he was shot three times in the head by Detroit police officers and pronounced dead on the scene, and he still lives today with no lingering cognitive dysfunction from the incident to date.

He's gentle, but not a pushover, please don't get it twisted. He'll go from zero to one hundred real quick. Over the years he's learned the power of the mind, how to manage it, and now he's teaching others how powerful the mind truly is. I've been telling him to write his book for years, so, Dad, if you're reading this, here's your reminder again to write the book.

My parents, my family all carried greatness, intellect, strength, and undeniable purpose. They gave me the best of themselves, yet even that couldn't protect me from the storms that found me. There are some lessons life assigns you firsthand, even when you come from love.

I was the little girl who was sexually molested and violated by family members (at the hands of people I trusted) —people I longed to know and be known by. I just wanted my family to love me for who I was, not for what they could take from me.

I was the little girl who was told to be quiet and slapped in the mouth several times because I always wanted to speak up.

I was the little girl who was always targeted by the mean girls who seemed to hate me because I merely existed.

I was the little girl who realized the more I achieved, the more I received attention and the more I was hated by other females.

I was the little girl who had big dreams, only for the adults around me to tell me I wouldn't amount to anything and that I couldn't save the world. I remember helping one of my uncles pull up watermelon from the field next to Gramp's house. I was at least a freshman in high school. I can't remember how the conversation went left, but I remember him telling me, "you'll be pregnant before you're out of high school and you won't amount to anything." And later as an adult, I remember being in the military and sharing with my mother how I wanted to help people. Get the homeless off the streets and help them transition back to normal life and I remember my mother telling me, "Baby you can't save everybody."

I was the little girl who didn't have her father growing up and found validation in relationships and learned the art of manipulation to survive life at an early age.

I was the little girl who watched her single mother do everything she possibly could to raise two little girls and not understand how to navigate the compass she was given to follow.

I was the little girl who lived in roach-infested apartments as a child and often woke up to something crawling on my skin, praying it wasn't the roach crawling on my bed. Not because my mother didn't keep a clean house (because she did, I've got the trauma to prove it, LOL), but because the roaches lived in the walls, and if there was pest control, they would only treat the living areas and not the areas and spaces behind the walls.

I was the little girl who went to every high school in our city except for one because rent increases wouldn't allow us to stay in any property longer than 12 months. My mother didn't finish the nursing program and didn't have a degree and the income she made doing hair, and taking care of 2 little girls while never really figuring out how to actually thrive financially unless we were living with my grandmother made us professional movers.

I was the little girl who was angry with the world for the hand she was dealt.

I was the little girl who was the target of a child molester and never understood why.

Was it my smile...
Was it my dimples...
Was I too nice...
Was it my body...

I was the little girl who hated so deep it should've been criminal.

I was the little girl who thought of suicide often and attempted it once as a child and once as an adult.

I was the little girl physically abused by a family member (not my mother) who lived in the house. So much so I wore long sleeves to school most of the 11th grade in the Florida heat to hide the scars so my mother wouldn't get in trouble.

I was the little girl who witnessed my beautiful, hard-working mother get beaten by someone who said they loved her. I witnessed, with rage, the brutal fights and jumping in to protect as I got older. I'll never forget seeing my mother being hit in the head with a walking cane. I did everything I knew how to protect her. I never understood why she kept going back.

I was the little girl who saw my mother being arrested for food-stamp fraud because she didn't make enough to make ends meet. But her income wasn't low enough for the state poverty level to receive food stamps. So she lied.

I was the little girl who slapped my Gramps because I was so fed up with years of hearing the way she fussed at me, made me feel unwelcomed most of the time and talked about my mother.

I was the little girl who humbly went into new environments (school, work, church as an adult), and no matter how I tried to hide and stay out of the spotlight, leadership always saw the assignment in me and elevated me, which resulted in more people hating me or being jealous. Favor hasn't always been fair for my life.

I was the little girl who had no respect for a man and vowed to never allow a man to be in a position to control me in any way.

I was the little girl who graduated high school and got on the first thing smoking to leave the entire state of Florida, a place I no longer felt safe in, but was expected to love.

These are the broken pieces of me served on a platter to let you know that it never stopped the assignment God has on my life. Delayed, possibly. I like to refer to it as marination. I was marinating.

Think about it, have you ever had an amazing, mouth-watering, rich piece of chicken, steak, pork, or even a turkey that was marinated to perfection? Sometimes the brining process takes hours, sometimes days, or even weeks. But once prepared and served, it's the best and most tender meat you've ever had in your life.

Ever wonder why aged cheese has a distinct, rich taste and is more expensive than the unaged cheese? Or for my fellow wine drinkers, the older the wine, the better the taste. And for the non-sipping saints, take a regular bottle of sparkling cider (any flavor or brand I prefer Welch's), don't open it and let it sit for a year. When you consume it, you'll have to look at the bottle twice to make sure it has no alcohol in it.

There's something about the marination or fermenting process, there's something about sitting in environments and allowing the ingredients or pressures of life to develop you into a fully marinated vessel. The vessel God can put on display, not because you're perfect but because you are willing and obedient.

Think about the last trial or storm you overcame. Not a current one. What took place? What did you learn? Who did you become as a result of learning the lesson? See, it's those pressures that prepare you for people, for ministry and also to conquer some of those fears. Based on some situations you've overcome, you received courage and now instead of shrinking (which was your default setting), you've learned how, what, and when to confront certain things. Also, facing your fears and trusting God and gaining faith at a level that was never possible (had it not been for those specific trials or obstacles). You can now face the next mountain or the next giant. See we're only as juicy and flavorful as our marination process.

Let me tell you...
You had to go through the divorce.
You had to lose that child.
You had to get fired.
You had to be molested.
You had to conquer cancer.
You had to be the target.
You had to lose it all.

You were chosen for such a time as this and while going through what you endured didn't feel good, it made you better. Not taking away from the trauma, because you deserved to be loved well. You deserved to be taken care of. You deserved to be celebrated. But Sis, if you didn't overcome, would you be who you are today? This very moment?

I remember the day I got the phone call from the hospital that my mother had died. I was giving my son a bath, excited about my mother's arrival to DC as it was a few days before her birthday and her gift was visiting DC. She was working, had received a phone call from her ex-husband (not my dad) that put her into cardiac arrest. She had a heart defibrillator to do the work of the heart when the heart couldn't function on its own so we never imagined there would be a moment her heart wouldn't beat. This moment. I dropped the phone and I vaguely remember anything else. I don't remember how my son got out of the tub, I don't remember who else I talked to. There are clips and glimpses of memories from that day and the next weeks ahead and it was literally the worst season of my life. It was as if someone had taken a balloon, used a needle to puncture a tiny little hole to prick the balloon for the air to slowly dissipate. I was numb for years afterwards. I even got angry with God because she died. Once I was able to endure the grieving process and heal, I was able to trust God like never before. While my situation is very different from someone else losing their mother, now there is a strand of familiarity I can relate to and serve someone else losing their mother from a true place of empathy because of that trial.

I had to be ready. Ready to no longer be the victim. No longer wanting to live in the sad story hoping someone would see me, save me, help me.

Now it's time for you to shift from the victim, walk through your healing so you can pour.

Still Not Convinced

Even after settling into this introduction, there's still a woman reading this who isn't quite convinced she's still the one God chose. Maybe you're thinking,

"That's for so and so, but not for me."
"I've made too many mistakes."
"I've disqualified myself."
"But, I'm divorced."

"But...but...but...but...but" until your butt falls off.

Sis, I got you. I was once you.

I know what it feels like to wear the weight of failure like a crown and believe that your story is too messy to be ministry. Yes, I know the Body of Christ has established a culture where when you sin or if you're not displayed as "perfect" a great level of shame and condemnation is thrown on you. Let me remind you, God doesn't call the flawless. He calls the willing. He calls the obedient. And throughout Scripture, He consistently used people the church would've written off and thrown the blanket of guilt and shame over.

Now, before I get canceled and banned from every church on earth, let me clarify that I'm not giving you permission to sin. I'm giving you permission to become without the blanket of shame and guilt. As long as we're here on earth, we're all working on something from the Pope to the Apostle to the lay member; no one is exempt, which means none of us is perfect. We're striving for perfection. Over the years, we've learned how to hide our sins really well and the higher the position we hold (because the judgement is real), the better we become at hiding our mess. This isn't an indictment on leadership or the church, these are facts that push people away from their calling and we have to do a better job and steward God's people better. You're not eliminated from your call from God because you sin; the reality is because you sinned or because of your flaws, it positions you for the call.

Think about it. If you're single and you struggle with fornicating, would you listen to the wisdom and guidance of someone who is married for 30 years and goes home to her husband every night for sex on how to stay abstinent? You might, but you might also receive it more from another single person who struggled with fornicating, who understands the feelings that come upon you at night, who understands the loneliness, the late night calls, and has overcome battle after battle after battle to remain abstinent.

Listen, sex is so GOOD. God created it and everything He creates is good. But it's supposed to be set aside and consecrated for marriage. Once you get the first taste of someone rubbing their fingers down the small of your back, kissing the valley of your navel, and working their way to fill you...okay, okay, I'll stop. Get yourself together sis, the point of the story is once you've experienced good sex, you desire it and want more of it. So when you're single and you desire sex and you're looking for a way of escape, sometimes talking to the married woman who goes home to her husband every night isn't the best option. The married woman or minister who's been with her husband for 20+ years may not know how you feel, she may not understand the struggles or the desires and could mishandle you or the situation that may push you away from God instead of bringing you closer to God. So, in this situation, I'm listening to the person who truly understands the pains, the desires, and can give me something practical to help me to overcome the struggles in real time and walk me through my deliverance process instead of telling me to just pray.

Prayer is amazing and it works, but faith without works is dead. There are specific things you need to do in addition to prayer that will help you overcome these struggles. So back to my point, the sin doesn't disqualify you, it positions you.

Let's take Peter from the Bible, one of Jesus' closest disciples and arguably the messiest one of them all. Peter was impulsive. Peter cursed. Peter cut off ears. Yet Peter was the only one who was able to identify Jesus as the Anointed One, the Son of the living God, the Messiah, the Christ when Jesus asked. Jesus then identified him as Peter or Simon Peter (changed his name) and then Jesus established him as the rock in which He would build his first church **and** then gave Peter the keys to heaven's kingdom realm to prevent on earth that which is forbidden in heaven, and to release on earth that which is released in heaven. And yet Peter still denied Jesus three times. Here's what's interesting to me, Jesus knew Peter was going to deny Him and He still established the first church with him as the rock. Jesus knew Peter was going to deny Him and Jesus still allowed him to be a disciple. Jesus knew Peter was going to cut Malchus' ear off and yet He still allowed him to be a part of His inner circle. That's *grace* on display.

Then we have the Samaritan woman at the well. She had five husbands and was shacking up with a man who wasn't hers. She didn't come looking for a ministry moment, she was trying to get some water without running into people who would judge her. But Jesus met her in the dry place and turned it into a divine appointment. He didn't shame her, He *revealed Himself* to her. Yes, he told her to go and sin no more, but it was her sin that positioned her as the first evangelist as she ran into her city telling others about the Messiah.

And let's not forget David (one of my favorites) — the shepherd boy turned king, the worshiper and warrior who penned psalms still healing and ministering to us today.

David was anointed, beloved... and also deeply flawed. He committed adultery. He orchestrated a man's death so he could take his wife. He made leadership decisions that cost lives. And yet—God still called him "a man after My own heart." Why? Because even in his mess, David always returned to God. He didn't hide behind pride—he repented. He didn't abandon the call—he humbled himself for the call, he humbled himself for the assignment.

He was a man after God's own heart.

Do you see the pattern here?

The world saw flaws—God saw the **future**.

They carried shame—God gave them **assignment**.

They tried to hide—God said, "**I still want you.**"

So let me say this plainly:

It doesn't matter how broken, bruised, or behind you feel.

God will still use YOU.

But you've got to give Him something to work with. And when I say "something" you've got to believe you're still worthy of purpose no matter what you've done, no matter what you've been through.

Even right now.

And yes, I know there's a group of people like the Pharisees and Sadducees who are hypocrites and can't see the beam in their own eyes because they're busy seeking or looking for the needles in everybody else's eyes. I had to give myself permission to know this and be okay being the target. If they did it to Jesus, what makes you and I different?

My Grandma used to tell me as a child, "Don't be concerned about what people say about you. People are gonna talk about you for the rest of your life baby, even when you're dead and gone." Grandma was right. And guess what, sticks and stones do hurt. I know they hurt. It's just marination.

Do you know there are demonic spirits assigned to distract you from your calling? There are also angels assigned to your life as well to protect you and to be divine intercessors on your behalf. It's not a coincidence the enemy started messing with your confidence as a child. There's no coincidence you were molested, you were adopted, you were told that you were ugly as a child, or told that you would never amount to anything. Or maybe that's not true for you, but something happened in your life that rocked your confidence. Something took place in your life that has you second guessing your worth. What was that something? Seriously, sit in this moment sis. What was the moment in your life that reshaped who you'd become?

True story. My daughter (who is 16 at the time of me writing this book) was such a jolly, happy, silly, outspoken little girl who we could count on being authentically herself. I call her my flower child. She dressed like Punky Brewster (while never even knowing who she was), and never cared about what others thought of her. I loved it so much! She was the version of me I wish I'd never lost. And I did my very best as her mother to cultivate and protect it. Then life happened right about 9 years old. She was never molested, Thank you, Jesus.

She's never been without, Thank you, Jesus. She's always been spoiled. She is our miracle baby, she's the youngest and she and my son are nine years apart. We went to South Korea for a little over a week for her sixteenth birthday. She's never had a sad story as it relates to parenting or household trauma.

But she experienced racism at the tender age of 9 years old. We had just moved from our townhouse into the new neighborhood, and the house I'd always dreamed of. She experienced racism at school for the first time in her life and didn't understand it. She couldn't understand why people hate people because of the color of their skin from teachers to the students. She couldn't understand how a police officer who is supposed to be friendly and also protect the people could kneel on a grown man's neck until he killed him could exist in the same world she lived in. Could breathe the same air she breathes. And as we navigated the space as delicately as we knew how to give her truth in a way a nine year old could process and also ensure she continues to judge people by their character instead of the color of their skin, it was the pivotal turning point for her. I saw my bubbly flower child slowly wither away as she sunk into depression. As she tried to navigate her thoughts and connect to something similar to her, she then started to hang around friends who compromised her values. When that group dismantled, it rocked her. We were patient, we prayed, we also found a great therapist, and now she's back to being my flower child as a teenager.

I wrote all of that not to just put her business out there (she gave me permission). But now that we're on the other side of that trauma for her young life, I asked her, "What happened? What was the moment that changed who you would become?" And she said, "the moment when I realized my life wasn't sunshine and rainbows." Our moments don't have to be the same, but there was a moment, and before you move forward, you need to identify the moment.

You Need a Yes and a Map

You don't need to have it all figured out. And you don't have to be perfect. But you ***do*** need to ***decide***.

And to decide is (***de*** - away from | ***Cide*** - to kill off) move away from or kill off anything that doesn't align with your decision or choice.

If you're deciding today to no longer be the victim of your story, so you can start your healing process, this means every time you see so...and..so, or every time that thought comes up about what someone else did to you, YOU have to decide not to be a victim. By the grace of God, I've overcome this and it will not define me. I take off the crown and the blankets of shame and guilt and I choose to thank God I didn't die in that season of my life. I thank God for keeping me. I thank God I can now speak my truth and help someone else come out of the storm. It's making the choice not to stay there. It's making the choice to shift the narrative. It's making the choice to do something different so you can expect different results.

PSA alert, sis, we never go through something for ourselves; it's usually for someone else, we're simply the vessel or the mouthpiece.

You need a **yes that moves**, not just a heart that hopes.

God may have given you the vision, but it won't manifest without your participation.

So yes, sis—this book is your **map**. But what good is a map if you never take the first step?

Your "yes" is what activates direction. It tells Heaven you're ready to stop circling the same mountains and start moving toward destiny.

No, you won't have every answer. But, you will have alignment. And in this next season, alignment matters more than achievement. Alignment matters more than hustle. Alignment matters more than anything else.

You don't need another sign. You don't need more time. **You just need to move**.

You were never created to live small, that's why you're so frustrated with yourself. You were never called to play it safe. And everyday you're playing it safe. Everyday you're hiding.

There is something **bigger** for your life, and deep down, you know it. This section? It's not about a book.

It's a breaking point.
It's a call back to courage.
It's a reminder that purpose is waiting, but it won't chase you down. ***You have to pursue it.***

And the journey starts with a decision.

Just start it, sis. Because you were made for something bigger.

My Life Poured Out

Affirmations

I am made for more
I say yes to the calling on my life
I will no longer delay what I know I'm designed to do
Fear does not get to lead me—obedience does
I don't need perfection, I need alignment
God has already gone before me
I am equipped, empowered, and made for something bigger
Today, I start

Midwife Moment

Now it's your turn to push, to breathe, to birth something from within.

1. What do you need to give yourself permission to do? Is it permission to release the fear, is it permission to step away from a relationship, is it permission to trust God more, is it permission to step into purpose?

I might be dating myself here, but do you remember in school when you needed a permission slip to go to the bathroom or take a permission slip home to get your parents to sign giving permission for you to go on the field trip, watch a certain movie, take a sex education class, or attend a black history assembly event (s) during black history month? Well Sis, you are about to be the author of your own permission slip.

My Life Poured Out

Write yourself a permission slip of what you need to do in order to step forward into what God is calling you to do. This is real simple, don't overthink this. Here's an example:

I (your name), give myself permission to forgive (person you need to forgive) for doing (whatever they did). I am choosing to let that go as it no longer hinders me.

Write as many on one piece of paper as you can think of then place it on the mirror in your bathroom so you can see it everyday as you're getting ready for the day.

Fear Wrapped in Strategy is Disobedience

> Fear doesn't mean stop. It means God's about to stretch something in you that's been sitting too small for too long.

- Temeka Thompson

Chapter 1

Fear has a way of dressing itself up in wisdom.

It'll sound like:
"Now isn't the right time."
"You need more research."
"Make sure everything's perfect first."

Let's call it what it is: ***fear wrapped in strategy is disobedience.*** And if we're not careful, we'll spiritualize fear and call it discernment. We'll call it "waiting on God" when really, God's been waiting on *us*.

Sis, this chapter is not about managing fear, it's about facing it. And let me start by telling you something personal: Fear nearly stole this book from you. Yep, this very one you're holding.

I questioned EVERYTHING.
My voice.
My story.
My ability to finish.
My worthiness to even write to women like you.

Fear doesn't always shout. Sometimes it whispers:
"*Who do you think you are?*"

And it whispered those words so long in my ear I started believing it. Then I realized, **fear isn't a signal to stop. It's a signal to *lean in*.**

Because where there is fear, there's often something powerful on the other side.

My mother died two days before her 46th birthday. She had cardiac sarcoidosis that went undiagnosed for years and by the time she was diagnosed properly her heart was too weak for a full heart transplant so we had to settle for every trial and alternative medicine option available. Because of her experience fear became my driver when it came to my health. For years after her death, any sharp pain or irregularity of my heart I was seeing a doctor. Anything that went wrong, my fears of dying would isolate my thoughts and I would immediately go into panic mode and start seeing all these specialists and have them run tests. After having kids my weight has fluctuated like a yo-yo and it's been hard for me to maintain a weight I've been comfortable with. The longer the battle the more medical challenges I faced: fibroid's, endometriosis, hypertension, pre-diabetes, brain fog, being tired all the time and even a tumor on my ovary.

As fear consumed my thoughts and I got older, the more my reality was looking like I too would die early. As I finish the final edits on this book, I am 41 days beyond my 46th birthday, and guess what, I'm going to live as long as God has me here to do the assignment I was born to fulfill!!!

I remember it was January of 2024. I sat in my doctor's office in tears because she told me she was going to have to prescribe something to regulate my blood pressure. For the past three years, it had been elevated, and now we were out of options. I love my doctor, she's been my primary off and on for over twenty years. We have this mutual understanding: I love her, I appreciate her, and I respect her education. She'll tell me what's wrong and what she recommends. I'll ask for alternatives, bring my research to the table, and somehow we'll meet in the middle to get me back on track. But this time, the blood pressure deal stumped me. None of the alternatives, none of the "meet me in the middle" approaches were working. And surgery was approaching fast. I needed my blood pressure regulated before I could have my hysterectomy.

You have to understand—hypertension and diabetes does not run in my family's bloodline. Anemia does, and I've had it most of my life. Neither my parents or my grandmother were overweight. So when I sat there hearing the words "prescription medication," it hit me hard. It felt like I was starting something new in my family's bloodline, and I hated it. I hated the thought of needing something to manage what I couldn't fix or control.

At that moment, it felt like a death sentence. Because prescriptions don't cure the problem—they manage it. And they bring a laundry list of side effects that make you question if the band-aid is even worth it. At the time, I was already undergoing iron deficiency treatment and mentally preparing for the surgery I had committed to—getting rid of fibroids I carried for at least twenty-five years. Fibroids had been hindering my quality of life, and because of—guess what?

Yep. FEAR. I put off surgery. I put off treatment.

Afraid of having to pay a lot of money to have the surgery.

Afraid of losing my job because I wasn't available when needed due to the recovery time.

Afraid nothing would get done around the house because I was the only one doing mostly everything.

Afraid of not having enough money to sustain our household during the recovery process.

Afraid of not making it out of surgery.

Fear had me in a chokehold , paralyzed, and had me suffering for years. Not moving, not believing at my full capacity, all while serving such a BIG AND AMAZING GOD!!

Something shifted in me around 44 or 45 years old. I made a decision—I was tired of being in pain, tired of living with a poor quality of life every month because I was scared to take care of myself. My blood pressure had become the cement wall standing in my way, blocking the very healing I was praying for. So, I went on a mission to remove everything standing between me and that decision.

Some might say the hindrances were a sign I wasn't supposed to have the surgery—but I didn't see it that way. I saw it as a test of faith. I conquered the anemia with iron supplements and food, and we finally got my blood pressure regulated with a prescription.

I had a partial hysterectomy with the most amazing doctor and his staff and surgery was a success. Yes it took longer than anticipated, but they unraveled over 5 ½ feet of fibroids from my uterus. Ya'll I'm only 5'1", I was carrying fibroids as tall as my height. No wonder why I was in so much pain. Recovery was a bear. It was the first real surgery I'd ever had, I didn't do well with anesthesia and I was so weak. I couldn't open a bottle of juice. After surgery, I vowed to myself that the next years would be the best years of health I'd ever have in all of my life.

I decided I would work out to gain my strength back. I decided I would release the unwanted weight. I decided I was going to conquer hypertension. And it hasn't been easy. The first gym and workout plan weren't a good fit for me, so I had to find one that was.

Eventually, I found a great gym and a great personal trainer. I gave him my vision and my desires, and because he sees what God is doing in me, he came into alignment with God's will for my life.

Then my grandmother's health started to decline, which meant travel was imminent, and I was afraid I'd get off track with my workout routine. I prayed, and again, made a decision. I talked with my trainer, and it didn't matter if I was traveling to see my grandmother, heading to a speaking engagement, a conference, or even vacation, he was locked in and ready for virtual sessions or accountability.

And let me pause for a minute to say: it matters who you have in your life in certain seasons. My trainer has been solid. There were times I didn't want to work out, times I was fighting my own personal battles, and he'd have his gospel playlist playing, sometimes that alone was all I needed. Other times, he'd speak an encouraging word right when I needed it most. And he's not only concerned about my well-being but my family's as well and I'm so grateful for his assignment in our lives.

I also asked for help. I asked my family back home if they had gym memberships with a free buddy pass or a gym that would allow me to pay for a day pass. And because I chose to conquer fear, my options were limitless.

I was fifteen pounds away from my goal weight, stronger than I'd been since leaving the Air Force. Then, about eleven months after my partial hysterectomy, I had this horrible pain in my lower stomach that sent me to urgent care, which sent me straight to the hospital. The diagnosis: a cyst on my ovary. I went back to my surgeon, we discussed options, and because I chose to conquer fear again, I made the decision to remove the right ovary.

After surgery, the pathology report determined it was a tumor—thank God it was benign. I often ask myself: had I waited because of fear again, what would've happened? I bounced back quickly, walking around and doing things the very next day. My recovery was faster than before because I'd been working out for the past year. In fact, I had to slow down, because mentally I was ready to go, but my body quickly reminded me I had undergone two major surgeries within 14 months.

Why did I share that?

Because sometimes fear will convince you that obedience will cost you everything, when in reality, it costs you nothing God hasn't already covered. Health-wise, the surgeries didn't cost me anything but my deductible, which I paid out of my health flex spending account that I contributed to every month. I had saved up enough leave from work and never lacked financially during either recovery. My team picked up my duties, nothing was missing, and both times I was welcomed back with open arms.

My family—my village stepped up, and nothing in or around the house lacked. Every need was met. Every prayer was answered. And I made it out to tell the story.

Fear Feels Real—But It's Not the Truth

Listen to me: Fear is *loud*, but it's also not real. It feeds off of what *could go wrong* and *starves* what *God says is already yours.*

Let's define fear. It's an unpleasant emotion caused by *the **belief*** that someone or something is dangerous, likely to cause pain, or a threat. I want you to really sit in this: fear is an unpleasant emotion caused by the **belief** that something is dangerous or threatening.

Did you catch that? It's caused by *belief*. Which means fear doesn't actually exist, it's something we imagine. Fear is a product of our imagination. We give it form. We give it power.

Let me make it plain. Maybe you heard about a burglary in your neighborhood. So you do what anybody would do, you take precautions, double-check the locks, make sure the lights are on, and go on about your business. But then...you start thinking about it too long.

All of a sudden, the place that once felt peaceful now feels uncertain. You start side-eyeing every shadow that moves under the streetlight. Every car that slows down feels suspicious. You find yourself getting up to check the locks—again. Your heart beats faster at the faintest sound, your breath gets short, and your mind starts playing entire Emmy award winning horror movie reels, scenarios that haven't even happened.

Then you hear something, a branch brushing against the window, or maybe a squirrel running through the leaves, and your heart is pounding so hard and fast like it's about to come out of your chest. And before you even realize it... fear has unpacked its bags and moved right in.

What was once your place of peace has now become a playground for anxiety. The burglary may have been true for someone, but it wasn't true for you. Still, you allowed the thought to grow until it took root in your mind. You gave life to something that wasn't even real for you; and now you've lost your freedom. That's what fear does. It builds a house in your imagination and convinces you to live in it.

Belief is a mental acceptance of something as true or real, often accompanied by conviction. It's subjective shaped by our own feelings, experiences, and perspectives. Which means sometimes, we create beliefs based on what others have said, what we've seen, or what we've watched on TV. And when those beliefs are rooted in fear, we end up producing our own reality, one that was never meant to exist.

Marisa Peer teaches that the mind's job is to do what it thinks you want it to do. In other words, the brain is the obedient servant of the mind, it doesn't analyze whether a thought is true, healthy, or harmful; it simply responds to what the mind tells it. So when you think something up good or bad your brain starts making it real.

And here's where most of us get stuck. We don't realize our thoughts are painting the picture that our faith, or our fear, will step into. What you continually think about eventually becomes what you expect, and what you expect becomes what you experience.

Now understand, you're not moving forward based on things that don't actually exist. You're afraid you'll get in front of people and not know what to say. Well you don't know that until you get in front of a group of people to speak.

You're afraid people won't want to listen to what you have to say. Well, you don't really know until you actually start talking to people. And the reality is, you probably talk to people every single day about something. But when you shape your thought process around something new or something you consider big, you're now afraid of it.

You're afraid you'll change if you get famous. Well, you don't really know until you become famous. And the reality is, you are who you are. More money or fame only magnifies who you already are.

So if you become selfish, that was already in your heart; it's just magnified by more.

You're afraid people will talk about you. Again, you don't know until you actually know. And the reality is, baby, people are already talking about you.

Fear is real for many people. The Bible doesn't ignore fear, it confronts it. That's why the command to "*Fear not*" is repeated over 365 times. God knew we'd wake up each day with something to fear—so He gave us a word to face it with.

Let's break it down:

- Fear of failure? **God's grace is greater (*or sufficient*).**
- Fear of rejection? **You're already accepted (*a chosen generation*).**
- Fear of not being enough? ***Sis, you were formed by more than enough (and you were wonderfully and fearfully created).***

Can we talk about Esther?

Homegirl was *terrified* to go before the king, rightfully so, it could've cost her her life. Still, she chose courage. She said, "If I perish, I perish." That wasn't a reckless statement, it was a faith-filled one. She was scared, but obedient and she moved anyway. That's called *facing fear with faith.*

Now let's pull in Gideon. One of my absolute favorites. God had to show me Gideon so I could see I wasn't the only one who was scared and asking for confirmation after confirmation. He was hiding in a winepress when the angel of God called him "*Mighty Warrior.*" And Gideon, he was like, "*Who, me?*"

Really think about this. A winepress built out of limestone, 20 to 30 feet underground for the process of making wine. Gideon was threshing wheat here, a place that wasn't designed to separate the wheat elements, a place that wasn't designed to separate the wheat from the tare (or the straw), a place that wasn't designed to get rid of the elements that didn't need to remain. Because he was afraid, a fear that had been passed down to him from his father he assumed the fear and then positioned himself in the fear.

Like many of us, his fear spoke first. His insecurity showed up strong. And his fear was generational. God didn't respond to Gideon's fear. He called out his **future**.

And that's exactly what God is doing with you.

He's not speaking to your fear. He's speaking to your **future.** To get there, you've got to go through fear, not around it. Joyce Meyer's book *Do It Afraid*, was the first time I realized I could do it afraid. It also reassured me that there are many powerful women that we admire today who were afraid at some point to step into the purpose God has for their life, but they still had to step. And once you actually take the very first step, you'll realize it wasn't as bad as you imagined it would be.

You Can Be Anointed and Afraid

Can I free you right here?
You can be called and still feel fear.
You can be anointed and still feel anxiety.
You can be appointed and still feel unsure.
None of that disqualifies you.

Courage isn't the absence of fear, **it's the decision to move forward in spite of fear.**

Obedience is what cancels fear's permission to control your future. God knew fear was going to be a big deal for a lot of people. That's why it's addressed so many times in the bible.

My calling comes straight out of Ezekiel 2–3. And because God knows me so well, He had to remind me again and again not to be afraid of their faces. God gave me this calling 26 years ago, that He was sending me to a rebellious nation, and I'm only supposed to speak what He gives me. The people are going to be stiffhearted. And these aren't the unbelievers; these are supposed to be people in the Body of Christ. He told me not to be afraid of their faces. If I didn't give the warnings and speak what He gives me and they die, the blood will be on my hand. But if I was obedient, I wouldn't have to worry about their blood on my hands.

Now can you imagine the dialogue I was having with God? LOL!!! Chile...Similar to Gideon, "Who me? What? The church being rebellious? The church worshiping idols?"

Yes, this was the exact charge God gave Ezekiel. But every single time I ask God about my purpose, my life, and what He wants me to do, He refers to this passage. Every. Single. Time. It never fails.

So when I say I had to marinate, I had to marinate and give myself permission to be judged by the very modern day Pharisees and Sadducees. And had I not endured what I've endured all of my life, I wouldn't be ready for this fully surrendered season.

I honestly didn't know how it was going to show up. In singing, in writing, in speaking, in coaching, in real estate, I just didn't know. So I moved and what I realized is **I am** the assignment. God shows up in every part of my life when I yield.

And to women? The way I've been mistreated by females my ENTIRE life? And God called me to them? To ya'll? Baby, I bucked...and I bucked...and I bucked.

I was like God are you serious?
You do remember the side-eye looks...
The way they came to my house to fight me...
The way they shoved me in the hallway...
The way they lied on me...
The way they talked about me...
The way they thought I wanted their men...

Lord, "*I don't be bothering nobody*" and they're always coming for me. You want me to go and talk to them?

Jesus, did He just say that? Are you interceding on my behalf with this one? Bro, help a sister out. I don't think He got this one right. I was literally having this conversation and several others all throughout the years. So I slowly stepped out to see if I was on track...

The more I stepped out, the more I wasn't sure I heard him right. My first women's conference crickets...

I had one friend and two women who were members of our church at the time show up. I did no massive advertising. So the following year, I did it again and the same thing, a total of 5 women including myself and the guest speaker. I was like, okay cool. Clearly I missed it. I won't do another one. No indeedy. It requires too much work, too much time, and effort for no one to show up.

My husband and I are founders of Marriage Takeover® where we help couples win in their marriage by identifying their triggers and breaking generational cycles. We launched a membership where we offer group coaching for the wives and husbands. While we were coaching the couples, I could still hide behind my husband, but then we noticed a need for the wives and husbands to meet separately so I was being pushed to pour into the wives by myself and I was terrified. God was saying, baby girl, you're done marinating.

Now I step forward (1) knowing that I already have the victory. Everything has already been won spiritually, I just need to walk through the manifestation. And every step gives me an opportunity to trust God more than I've ever trusted him before. (2) I know I'm not fighting alone. God is with me. I ask for confirmation after confirmation. And God reassures me He's with me. That doesn't mean I won't take the hits, because I will. That doesn't mean bad won't hit my life, because it does, but God is with me so, I don't have to fold in any situation. If I lose a job, if a family member dies, I know He's got me. And there's something He wants me to learn through whatever experience He allows me to face. So now, ***we step***. And what God has proven to me over and over again, something I can bet my life on, is when we take a step, He's given me the provision before my foot lands on the ground. And (3) I lead with my flaws. I learned a long time ago that you can beat Satan to the punch; by removing fear, shame and guilt. How do I do that? We all know what our flaws are, we know the negative self chatter we tell ourselves that keeps us stuck. I lead with that, it's not a secret.

I don't know if you've ever experienced seeing spit come from a speaker's mouth as they are preaching or speaking. Or even been baptized by someone's spit because they spit when they talk. I've seen it, I've witnessed it and I have to say I even do it. And there is nothing worse than to be listening to someone and you feel that wet sensation from someone else's mouth, it's disgusting. So if I'm in close proximity to an audience, I'll say, "Listen, I spit a little when I talk, so you may want to give yourself some room if you don't want to get baptized with my spit." I get a little laugh from the audience, they open up, some move some don't, but it also disarms me and gives me the ability to hear from God clearly and not be distracted by the thought of me spitting on someone and what they'll think. I've gotten to the point in my life where nothing will hold me back from doing what God has commissioned me to do.

So if God gives me a prophetic word for someone, I'll lead with, "This may not mean anything to you, but this is what I believe God is saying..." and leave it at that. And every step I take trusting Him, He shows me and guides me. He's never left me. Now, I've left him, but He's never left me.

The truth is, God knows some of us are going to be afraid. He's pushing us to trust Him more in the process. The more I trust God, the more God proves himself and we walk through fear together.

So yes, your knees might tremble.
Your voice might crack.
You might feel unqualified.
Move anyway.
Because the only way out of fear, is through it.

My Life Poured Out

Affirmations

I will not let fear dictate my destiny.
I am bigger than my insecurities.
I can feel fear and still move forward.
God goes before me, and I will follow.
My calling is louder than my doubt.
Today, I silence fear with faith.
I was born for boldness.
I face fear—and I win.

Midwife Moment

Now it's your turn to push, to breathe, to birth something from within.

1. Think about it, what fears are stopping you right now?
2. What beliefs shaped that fear? Was it something you experienced? Something someone told you? Something you watched? What was it?
3. Now instead of imagining something wrong or bad, imagine something good will actually happen.

Then take one step forward to conquer one fear each week, each month, or each quarter. Baby steps.

Come out of Hiding

> "People connect with your strength. But they heal through your scars. Every time you speak, someone else gets to live."
>
> - Temeka Thompson

Chapter 2

There's a reason the enemy wants you silent. If he can convince you your struggle disqualifies you, you'll never realize that your story is someone else's survival guide.

Let me say it a little more clearly: Your breakthrough isn't just for you. It's for every woman waiting to hear they're not alone.

But sharing our struggles? Whew—it's raggedy.
It's exposing.
It's vulnerable.

It's easier to dress it up, post the highlight reel, slap a Scripture on the wound, and keep it pushing. But healing doesn't happen in hiding. It happens in honesty, in vulnerability.

Your Struggle Has Strategy

For the longest time, I thought I had to get through the storm before I could speak. That I needed a pretty bow on the story before it was worth sharing.

But the Holy Spirit arrested me one day and whispered: *"They don't need your perfection, they need your process."*

During an event where I was singing, I shared that I was molested for the very first time. I was so afraid to do it before that moment. The holy spirit was flowing and it just came out. I looked at myself after I said it like "girl did you just say that?" I was talking about my healing, my forgiveness journey all centered around that pivotal point in my life. I think I sold more CD's that night than any other night because other women saw themselves through a moment of not being alone in being molested. What you've overcome has shaped you, but it doesn't define you. You are not your mistakes, you are not your failures. And the reality is because you didn't die in it, another woman, person or child is waiting to hear they don't have to die in it either.

I remember listening to Yolanda Adams when she had her radio show on Radio One. One morning she shared that she used to hate listening to herself sing, she didn't like her voice. She would record, but didn't like to go back and listen. THE YOLANDA ADAMS, who has a powerful, soul shattering voice that will break yokes when you're in the presence of her singing as God is flowing through her Yolanda. Her words blessed my entire life when she said that. It gave me some hope.

Now I don't sing like Yolanda (only in the amphitheater of my shower maybe), but to hear her be vulnerable with so many people listening and the dynamic voice she carries. It blessed me, I connected with her more and I wanted to learn more about her. I grabbed onto hope that day and didn't give up on my singing. I know I don't have the best voice, I have pitch and key problems.

We grew up singing, but I didn't grow up "sanging." I was well into my 30's before I knew there was a thing called a Vocal Trainer who could help you understand your voice and teach you how to use it at its capacity. I had no idea. Although I was the oldest, I grew up in the shadows of my younger sister who is drop-dead gorgeous and has the voice of an angel. She is absolutely amazing at singing and has sung all over the world. It was actually her everyone thought would have a CD out, not me. Not sure why she still hasn't dropped one yet (Sis, if you're reading this, what are you waiting for?). There is a nation of people waiting to hear your beautiful voice.

I was sitting in our townhouse on Eielson Air Force Base (AFB) in Alaska and writing in my journal praying and begging God if He'd just anoint my voice, I would sing for Him. I had a desire to sing, but nobody would take me seriously. And one day, God did it. He anointed my voice. Please don't misunderstand, I still get pitchy and I'm still off key and I have to work much harder to ensure I'm training my ear. But when the Holy Spirit is flowing, I'm not concerned with any of that and healing can actually take place. I know the gift of healing flows through my voice. And I had to overcome what others have told me and how it made me feel when it comes to singing to make room for the Holy Spirit to flow. As I depend on Him CDs were sold out, free gigs started coming, then paid bookings started to come, then music awards, then traveling all throughout the U.S. and internationally.

When people saw that I was human, when they could relate to me, when they could see themselves in my shoes, that's when ministry started taking off for me.

Now I'd done my due diligence with gathering all of the radio stations paying royalties, the producers and music director contacts, magazine editor contacts, all the things. I even had a marketing strategy and I saw a little success from the marketing push, but it wasn't until I yielded to the moment of my testimony. And at that time, I wasn't fully healed, I was still going through my healing process. But I submitted to the Holy Spirit and that was my success strategy.

The world is so tired of seeing what's fake, what's conjured up, they really want to see something real. They want to latch on to true hope. They want to know you see them, that you know what it's like to be them, and also be humble enough to connect with them.

Many of us have seen or played church and now we're really ready for more. I was a holiday saint. I fellowshipped on Easter, Hallelujah Night for Halloween sometimes, Christmas, and sometimes Vacation Bible School. I don't remember my mother taking us often, but I do remember my uncle Jerome taking us.

My mother used to sing in the choir when I was younger, so I remember moments of being in the sanctuary with her. What stands out most is sitting in the back of my uncle's Volkswagen Beetle with my white stockings or ruffle socks, my slip and dress, and those cute little black Sunday shoes with the strap across the front. I'd watch the Deacons line up the hymnals, then step outside afterwards to smoke. Those same men I'd hear later at family functions, cussing, mistreating, and talking about others.

The older I got, the less I went to church. I do remember being baptized the summer I turned fourteen, back in the old Baptist congregation where you had to go and tell everyone you'd gotten saved or been baptized. I honestly thought life was supposed to be rainbows and sunshine after that because I had given my life to Christ. I wasn't told temptations would get stronger, that trials might increase, or even in trouble, I'd have help walking through it. Instead, it felt like life got worse.

Years later, I got married. My husband used to say he'd been dragged to service as a child, so finding a place of worship was important to him. Miles away from our family in Alaska, where we didn't think Black families or churches even existed off the military base, we eventually found a place where we thought we could grow together spiritually.

This home church added to my already shattered view of what the house of God was supposed to look like, because the leaders mishandled God's people. I didn't really know how to be a wife back then. Our pastors at the time had been married for years, and Eric looked to them as examples—we needed the help. I didn't cook to his taste, I didn't honor him the way he needed, and our communication was a hot mess. We fussed and fought all the time, there was no peace. So I scheduled a session for us to meet with our pastors.

After talking with them, not only did the pastor's wife share our private business with other members (who didn't need to know what was going on in our home), but she also started prepping her youngest daughter to fill in the gaps for Eric. She was giving him extra greetings, baking cookies, and handing them straight to him. And y'all, I wasn't saved

SAVED. Long story short, when I found out what was going on, I confronted the mother and the daughter and let them know (not so nicely) if they kept trying to put a wedge in my marriage, I would tear up their house. And I told Eric, "Eat another got damn cookie if you want to, and I'll shove it down your throat and make sure you choke to death." I told you, I wasn't saved-saved.

The worst part was when we got home. Eric thought I didn't handle it right and said I owed them an apology. Then he told me I was carnal-minded. Now, I had my share of insecurities, and when it came to my husband, ministry, and my relationship with God, that was another layer, because he knew so much, and I looked up to him in that area. For the one I loved, the one who moved across the country to be with me, the one who I thought we'd conquer the world with, the one I admired in the house of God, the one I was taking care of—to tell me I was carnal-minded and needed to apologize...I felt like the whole world was against me. I hadn't felt that kind of isolation since I left home in Florida.

I'm built a little different ya'll and I will no longer apologize for it. I refused to apologize. I knew they were wrong and I was tired of being convinced there was something wrong with me. I showed up one last time before walking away from the congregation. That night, I prayed, "God, if this is what You call church, I don't want any part of it. Nope, you can have it. I'm good. I'll go back to the life I had before I ever knew what church was. Because there's got to be more than this. You can't tell me THIS is all You've got for Your people. I'll pass".

And it was right there in that raw, honest moment that my life shifted spiritually. That's when God started to show me the difference between *relationship and religion*. The difference between *Jesus* and the *Pharisees and Sadducees*. The difference between what's *authentic* and what's *not*.

In that moment, I felt like a toddler safe in the arms of the master keeper. God gave me a surety that I wasn't crazy, He opened my eyes. I felt seen for the first time, I felt heard for the first time. And I was open to letting go so I could experience more of His presence and truly learn more about having a relationship with Him.

Worship became my love language and that was the space where God and I met often. I learned how to lay broken before Him. I learned how to show up broken before Him and mendable before His people.

Yes, I left the home church. Eric continued to go and he'd bring home the bible study lessons for me to learn because I was so "carnal minded." God was showing me something in the teachings. He was showing me how to actually study, how to break the word down and He was giving me revelation of the word. So much so, I was showing Eric where he was getting his spiritual food from and how they were taking it out of context. But he couldn't see it coming from me, because I didn't know as much as he knew. I learned how to pray differently and I said, "God you show him." And when God started to show him, he would humbly come back and apologize. That season taught me something powerful, it taught me how to war in prayer and worship quietly, even when misunderstood. Because externally, before the people, I let them see my scars, but internally, in my home, I let my husband see my wounds, the very wounds he made. Worship became my gateway. Now

27 years later we're pastoring together.

Sis, there is power in letting people see you *in it.*
Not just after the victory.
But during the tears.
During the questioning.
During the stretch.

You think people connect with your strength, but they heal through your scars.

And when you share your struggle? You take the shame out of it. You expose the enemy. You gain strength and courage. You free yourself and you free someone else who's been battling silently, thinking they were the only one.

Paul wrote most of the New Testament, casting out demons, raising people from the dead...and still admitted, "*There's a thorn in my flesh.*" He could've kept it hidden. Instead, he *shared it.* Why? Because Paul knew power is made perfect *not in strength*, but in weakness. And when he exposed the struggle, we gained a theology of grace.

His strength is made perfect in our weakness. It's not until we're weak, when we no longer have the capacity that we make room for God to come in and move. And when He moves, that's when the miracle takes place, because it can't be done in our own strength.

Hannah, desperate for a child, praying with such anguish that people thought she was drunk. She didn't hold it in. She poured out her soul. She desired a child and she was barren. And her raw honesty and

and perseverance birthed the prophet Samuel. Her struggle of being barren didn't stop the promise. It pushed it into motion. And she didn't care who saw it.

The World Doesn't Need More Perfection, it Needs More Permission

As a daughter of the King, I get sick to my stomach when I see what "church" has become and what we've made it to be. People are tired of a watered-down experience of His presence. They don't want performance; they want presence. They want a relationship that's real. They want to know God sees them. They want to know God cares. They want to know there's hope. They want to know that God is really real.

But when you're too busy judging people...
When you're competing over members and money...
When you're married but sleeping around with your members, men and women alike...

When your heart isn't postured right before God, they can't see Him through you.

When you share your struggle, you don't glorify the pain.

You glorify the God who carried you through it.
You glorify that God is real.
You glorify that God cares.
You glorify that God still heals.
You glorify that God is still a miracle worker.

This isn't about trauma dumping, it's about truth-telling. It's about testifying in real time, even when the tears haven't dried yet. And yes, there will be some who mishandle you and your testimony.

Remember, this is all part of the marination process. God is seasoning your story for someone else's freedom. It's because of what I experienced that I'm able to understand the word of God for myself. It's because of what I've experienced that I don't have a problem with saying something's not right to leadership. It's because of what I've experienced that I can't be manipulated by the word of God. It's because of what I've experienced that I can't be manipulated from the pulpit.

So, know *every time you speak, someone else gets to breathe.* I'm going to even say this Sis, every time you speak, someone else gets to live.

So open your mouth.
Tell your story.
Share your struggle.
And let God turn your ashes into an altar.

Not for people to worship you, but for them to experience Him in a way they never thought was possible.

My Life Poured Out

Affirmations

I am not ashamed of my journey
What tried to break me only revealed the strength inside me
My voice is valuable
My process is powerful
I won't wait to be perfect
I show up now in truth
God gets the glory even in my groaning
My story is a healing sound for someone else
Today, I speak, even if my voice shakes

Midwife Moment

Now it's your turn to push, to breathe, to birth something from within.

1. What struggle have you been hiding because you feared judgment? Write it down. Be honest. Name it.
2. What do you wish someone had told you while you were in the thick of it? Now write that down for someone else.
3. Who is one person who would be encouraged by your story, if you had the courage to share it? Write out the first sentence you'd say. Speak to them with empathy and power.

Pray this:
God, use my pain to heal others. Let my process become someone else's permission. Let your oil pour over me, and through me. Give me wisdom, boldness, and humility as I speak with truth and grace so someone else will know that you're still real, that you're still alive and that you still do miracles. In Jesus Name Amen.

What feels like the wilderness might be the womb

"Purpose doesn't promise easy. But it does promise impact."

- Temeka Thompson

Chapter 3

I struggled with whether this chapter should even be in this book, or if it should be a completely separate one. Because this section is for the daughter, for the woman who's finally realizing she's been called, flaws and all, and has started facing her fears head-on taking the necessary steps into purpose.

She is getting honest about her story. She gave God her yes, shaky, but surrendered. But, I also didn't want to delay this part of the book for the woman who's already given herself permission with a heart that's fully surrendered. And I didn't want the book to feel incomplete or cut short. So here we are. This is the part nobody warns you about.

See, we love the idea of walking in purpose, until the ground gets a little unstable. Until things don't go according to plan. Until the warfare gets real, the support gets silent, and you start asking, "*God... did I miss it?*"

I told you previously in this book, I did two Women's Conferences (actually I think it was 3) and in my eyes it wasn't a big success. Each time spending money, time and effort for no more than 10 people to show up. After the very last event, I lost a good friend because they didn't understand my testimony had nothing to do with them. They thought I used the pulpit to call them out and that was not the case at all. Even after trying to explain, apologizing, and letting them know my heart's intent, our relationship has never really been the same as it was before that event. So again, I'm like God, clearly I missed it.

Two years after my last conference, the one I swore I would never do again—I ran into a lady at a community event about financial literacy and estate planning. My husband and I had gone to meet with an attorney to review our trust documents, and as we were finishing up, a woman stopped me and said, "Hey!!!"

Now, if you know me, I'm going to return that same energy, but I had no idea who this lady was. I smiled and said, "Hey! How are you doing?" She said, "You remember me?" I honestly didn't, and I didn't want to lie, so I told her, "I see so many people, help me remember."

She said, "You did a women's conference called *Warrior Woman*. It blessed me so much, I still have my battle kit." And I almost cried. Because where I didn't feel like it was successful, where I had told God what I wasn't doing anymore, that very event had left such a mark on her she remembered it two years later like it was yesterday.

She told me she'd been following me on social media, but I had no idea, because I wasn't active. I wasn't showing up the way God wanted me to because it was hard, because I was frustrated. In that moment, I remembered her, asked about her family, and my husband was standing there grinning ear to ear. He was leaping and laughing with joy, because he's my #1 fan in everything especially ministry. For him, it was an answered prayer.

Let me help us out Sis, ***purpose doesn't promise easy. But it does promise impact.*** Impact always comes with pressure. The greater the pressure, the greater the power behind it.

Think about it, diamonds aren't born in comfort; they're formed in deep places, hidden beneath the surface, where nobody can see what's happening. Down in the earth's mantle, with immense heat and the pressure is relentless. Over time, pressure and heat begin to transform ordinary carbon into something extraordinary. What was once common becomes rare. What was once overlooked becomes invaluable.

And here's the thing—it doesn't happen overnight. It takes time. Years. Millions, sometimes even *billions* of years. That's what I call the *marination process.* It's not quick and it's not easy.

Constant heat and pressure is not meant to destroy you, it's designed to develop you. It's how God bonds every piece of who you are into something unbreakable, something beautiful, something brilliant, something rare.

Where you feel like all hell is breaking loose because of the pressures of life, it might mean this is the great force designed to produce your level of impact. And remember it's not about you. I know that's hard to wrap your brain around when you're actually going through it. When I finally realized it wasn't about me, anytime I was going through the worst trials of my life, I kept telling myself, "Temeka, this isn't about you. There is a couple who needs to know they can make it on the other side of this." or "There is someone who needs to know they can overcome this. Stay focused. God's got you." And again I would find myself in worship for direction, worship for wisdom, worship for strength.

Your "Yes" still comes with a Cross

Somewhere along the way, I started believing this lie that if I'm in purpose, everything should align smoothly. Doors will fly open, people will cheer, and I'll feel peace all the time.

Nah, sis. Buckle-up Beau.

Sometimes walking in purpose looks like crying on the bathroom floor after obeying God. Sometimes it looks like doing the right thing and still getting attacked. Sometimes it looks like being broke, broken, and still booked to speak. Hard times don't mean you're out of purpose or not in alignment. Sometimes, it means you're deeper in it than you've ever been. Where I've been celebrated in the spotlight, the same spotlight was also the target.

Let me be transparent: launching *Daughter Arise* ™ (formerly known as My Life Poured Out) was one of the most purpose-filled—and pressure-packed—assignments I've ever walked out. It didn't come during a season of ease. It wasn't born in a moment where I had unlimited time, energy, and clarity. I was exhausted. Life was lifing and literally falling apart. Spiritually, I was being stretched. Personally, I was carrying a lot. I knew, deep in my spirit, this was something God had planted in me. Not for *later*, but for *now*.

There were so many moments where I second guessed everything.

Am I really called to this?
Will women show up?
Can I carry this without losing myself?
Is it the right timing?

Here's what I learned ***when you pour from a surrendered place, God provides the oil.***

What started as a trembling yes turned into transformation for every woman who showed up. I watched women weep, heal, confront lies, rediscover purpose, and find sisterhood in a way that still brings tears to my eyes. And none of it would've happened if I had waited for the storm to pass.

When my mother passed away in August of 2002, I slowly stopped going back home to Florida. I made a trip the following year, around Thanksgiving, and the pain was so heavy it silenced something in me. The grief was raw. I found it easier to just stay away.

Life kept moving. Our son got busy with sports, work consumed my days, and holidays began to take shape around the family we were building in Maryland. Traditions shifted. What were once annual visits became every few years... and then a decade passed in what felt like a blink. My family back home knew us mostly through pictures and posts on social media. Many of them had never even met our daughter in person. Something changed in 2023, I looked at my grandmother and saw time catching up with her. Her voice, her posture, the way her body moved all spoke louder than words. I knew it was time to go back more often. When I returned, I told Eric I wanted to start going home at least every six months. No hesitation, he supported it, and he made space to make it happen. Each visit felt different. My grandmother's health declined rapidly. She was weaker every visit. Slower. And deeply in need of attentive care.

I sat down with my aunt and uncle (her caregivers) and asked simple but direct questions. What were the doctors saying? What was she eating? What medications or supplements was she on? I didn't ask to take over, and I wasn't trying to disrespect the care they'd been giving. Caregiving is no small task, I know that, and I honor it. Truth is, I saw things I couldn't unsee.

I'm someone who believes in holistic care, naturopathic health, organic eating, healing through God's food first. I prefer a natural supplement over a prescription drug any day. But there comes a point when something isn't working, it's time to shift the plan. And when that shift doesn't happen? At some point, it becomes neglect. It became clear to me some answers weren't forthcoming. And the choices being made...I didn't agree with. I wasn't a child anymore. I was a full grown woman with children, still being seen as a child. And I'd grown to approach life differently. Still, I knew there was only so much I could do. I couldn't rewrite the whole narrative. I couldn't force change. So, I did what I could: I showed up. I listened. I advocated quietly. I prayed fiercely. And I loved my grandmother in every way I knew how, with presence, patience, and honor.

When I saw my grandmother Labor Day of 2023, I took her to the beach for the first time. She was 89 years old and had never been to the beach. So I took her to Panama City beach and then afterwards we had breakfast and I allowed her to eat whatever she wanted to eat. Dementia was slowly deteriorating her mental capacity, but she knew what she wanted to eat. And she ate all of her food and used her finger to wipe the plate clean, LOL.

While it brought me great joy to see her so happy, I was also so very angry to see she wasn't getting enough food and nutrition. I had long conversations with the in-home healthcare specialist who showed so much love and respect for my grandmother. I was devastated seeing my grandmother in April of 2024, the difference seven months make when you don't receive the proper nutrition. I offered to help, I offered to sit in and give relief to the caregivers and to no avail.

I remember a moment that still sits heavy on my heart. We had all gone out as a family to eat at a restaurant. After the meal, my grandmother—still sharp, still full of grit wanted to walk a bit, take in the atmosphere, and greet people the way she often did. She moved slowly, yes, but intentionally. She was present. I didn't mind at all. I welcomed those moments, because I understood the beauty in them. Not everyone agreed.

On the way out, I witnessed something that made my spirit ache. As my grandmother tried to move at her own pace, she was abruptly ushered forward by a family member. With a sharp fierceness in her voice, she said, "Stop pushing me. Why are you always pushing on me?" It took everything in my sister and I not to say something at the moment. Instead, we gently walked alongside her. We let her take her time. We let her speak. We let her live. And we stood in the moment with her, because we understood how sacred that space was.

In those few seconds, my grandmother told us everything without saying much at all. We saw it clearly. She wasn't being cared for in the way she deserved. And my heart broke, not just out of anger, but out of deep love for a woman who had given so much for her family, only to be mishandled in her later years.

Between Purpose and Pain

I honestly felt like a soldier on the front lines of a spiritual battleground, dodging bullets in the air and land mines on the ground. I was praying constantly, praying for my grandmother to be cared for, praying not to let resentment take root, praying for grace to forgive, and begging God not to let hatred harden my heart. I didn't want to carry that kind of weight. And in the middle of all of it, God was thrusting me into my purpose. I was launching **My Life Poured Out**—a movement where I help women discover their identity and walk boldly into what God created them to do. I had just wrapped the most incredible brand photoshoot I'd ever had. I worked with a coach who saw me and the mandate God has over my life. I was finally stepping out from behind the shadows of my husband and into the light of my own anointing. We had built something beautiful together with *Marriage Takeover* ™, but now God was saying, "*This next part is for the women.*"

And as I was rising in excitement and clarity... until I received a text that knocked the breath out of me.

We were about 20 minutes outside of Columbia, SC when my aunt messaged me that Gramps had fallen at home and was rushed to the hospital. It felt like the wind had been snatched from my lungs. Everything around me stood still (although we were going about 80 mph on the highway). I couldn't breathe. I couldn't think. It was like I was standing still and everything around me was moving in slow motion.

I called for more details, there were none. Gramps was at home with her now third or fourth new healthcare provider. There was a new one every visit home. To this day, no one knows exactly when she fell or how long she was unconscious on the floor. And yet, I had a major launch scheduled within a week. I was supposed to be preparing to pour into women. To speak life, purpose, and healing over them. But inside? I was asking God:

"Are you sure I'm supposed to be doing this? Are you sure this is the right time?"

Because every time I move forward, it feels like my world falls apart. It was a roller coaster of emotions, one minute up, the next minute I'm plummeting and low-crawling to safety. And the spiritual tension?

Unbearable.

When I got to Florida, I saw my grandmother in a coma. I had only seen one other person in a coma then, I was on assignment as a minister at my local church to pray with the family and be with the family. This time...it was my family. My heart felt like it was breaking into tiny little pieces. Each fissure gave me a new ache I couldn't describe. I couldn't believe this was my life. As if that weren't enough, while I was there, my great-uncle (Gramp's brother) passed away. A man I'd known and loved my entire life. We had celebrated with him in Florida two weeks earlier.

And now... it felt like loss was circling us.

Despite the grief, I was relieved my grandmother was finally in the hospital receiving nourishment, care, and rest. She weighed only 98 pounds. I had *never* seen her that small in my life. And I knew, in the depths of my soul, if she recovers and is sent back home, it would be the end of her days on this side of the dirt.

I stayed with her for a week. She began to show small signs of improvement. And when I left to return home to my family, I held onto the hope that as long as she remained in the hospital, she had a fighting chance.

But the truth underneath all of this? The tension with her care. Gramps had siblings who lived within walking distance, siblings who hadn't been allowed to see her since the COVID pandemic began. She wasn't being nourished properly. For years, only a strict list of "approved foods" were allowed: bean soup, bananas, cottage cheese, green drink supplements, and water mixed with other powders. No one else was allowed to cook for her. No one else could advocate for her. Even doctors were being misled, prescriptions were swapped out for supplements. Health decisions were made without accountability, and years of that routine were catching up with her. This wasn't mismanagement. It felt like neglect. And her rapid decline showed it.

I remember one moment so vividly. My sister and I were cutting up bananas for one of my aunts who was wheelchair bound in the house when we noticed Gramps reaching for the fruit. She was hungry trying to quietly take a piece of banana from her daughter's hand. I had to ask the caregiver: "*When was the last time she ate? What did she have?*" We immediately gave her bananas. She ate like someone who hadn't been fed. Ya'll I could've exploded.

The last time I visited her in April before she went into a coma, she had fallen out of a single sofa chair. I rushed to help her up. And as she reached for me, she mouthed the words:

"**Help me.**"

I'll never forget the look in her eyes—pure despair.

That night and a few nights after that, I cried myself to sleep. And I realized...she wasn't just asking me to help her up.

She was asking me to rescue her.
To love her.
To feed her.
To care for her in the way her dignity deserved.

The moment still lives in me. And it's part of the reason I keep showing up for women through what started as *My Life Poured Out* that turned into *Daughter Arise*™. Because if I could do nothing else, I could be a safe place for someone else's mother. Someone else's daughter. Someone else's inner *little girl.*

And I can hear you saying, "That couldn't have been my grandma. I would've reported them. Why didn't you report them?"

And as much as I questioned family decisions, my heart still carried compassion. And as crazy as it sounds, I honestly believe the family members thought they were doing the best thing for them.

So I did what I could.
I visited more.
I called more.
Asked better questions.

I sat with every caregiver who entered the house. I asked them about their instructions, what they observed, what they were told to do. I watched. I listened. I showed up. And when I was home, I made sure Gramps and my aunt ate. I tried to bring peace and joy into a house with every visit where so much had gone unspoken. I believe Gramps felt that energy. That shift. That presence. Whether in her home... or in the hospital. Because she asked me to help her. And even when she fell into a coma and had been unresponsive for two days, she still knew when her granddaughters showed up. My sister and I arrived on day two, and we went to work. Not only as granddaughters, but as daughters of the Most High.

We knew the power of God's presence.
We played worship music.
We prayed over her body.
We talked to her like she was awake.
We touched her gently and spoke life.
We filled the hospital room with love and light.

And she started responding. Physically and spiritually.

I believe her spirit knew she was safe with us in the room. That she wasn't alone. That heaven was near, and we were holding the line. Eventually, I had to return home. My husband and I had an anniversary trip planned with friends in Las Vegas, and I prayed she would hold on.

She did. She held on through my anniversary, and two weeks later, she passed. We received word the hospital was preparing to discharge her...and shortly afterward, she was gone. Still trying to balance ministry, family, grief, and calling. I postponed my My Life Poured Out launch until the second week of June to accommodate funeral plans. But let me tell you April through June were heavy. There was loss. There was heartbreak. There was unforgiveness and bitterness that tried to root itself in my spirit.

I'll spare you the chaos surrounding Gramps' funeral arrangements because that chapter could be a book of its own.

But even with all of it...**the assignment didn't stop.**

Because when God puts purpose in your belly, grief can't cancel it.

Disappointment can't delay it.

Family dysfunction can't derail it.

I learned how to hold pain in one hand and purpose in the other.

How to weep and still pour.

How to forgive and still lead.

How to lose and still obey.

And that's surrender on full display.

Through the hard times, the assignment was still present.

Through the hard times, the call was still present.

Through the anger, the assignment was still present.

Through the bitterness, the call was still present.

Through sitting at the hospital, laying beside my grandmother, rubbing her face, seeing the despair in her eyes, the assignment was still present.

I had my first launch and it was a success. I then scheduled another launch in October. Guess what, my aunt who was living with my grandmother passed away. Then another one of my aunt's unexpectedly passed away in December of 2024. In total my husband and I had 6 family members to gain their wings, 4 on my side and 2 on his side. We still had to serve, our assignments never stopped.

MLPO was born in the *middle* of a hard time. And that's how I know it was God. Because purpose that only works in comfort isn't purpose, it's convenience.

So sis, I'm telling you from experience; *what feels like a wilderness might be the womb. Don't abort the mission.*

People often don't know the cost of your oil. So before you talk about your pastor or your leader, first consider their cost.

Through having their own family turmoil, they still serve;

Through their own financial ruins, they still serve;

Through their own health challenges they still serve;

Through their own grieving, they still serve;

They officiate funerals while still grieving themselves;

Through not getting enough rest (because they're all things to all people), they still serve.

And many of them serve so well you'll never know they're going through their own trials.

The cost of your purpose is showing up when you're going through.

Joseph had a dream straight from God, but life didn't match the vision.

He was Betrayed.
He was Sold.
He was falsely Accused.
He was Forgotten.
He was Locked up.

If you judged his purpose by his circumstances, you would've sworn he was cursed. But Joseph never lost sight of the promise. And in the pit, the prison, and the palace, he carried the same posture: Faith. And received a great reward.

Then there's Ruth. She lost her husband. Left her home. Followed her grieving mother-in-law to a foreign land. That doesn't sound like purpose, it sounds like survival. But what looked like loss was actually divine positioning. In the middle of gleaning in a field, she found favor, legacy, and alignment.

What am I saying?

Purpose will pull you through pain before it reveals the promise. So if it feels hard right now, don't back up.

Lean in.
Lean in to what God is showing you.
Lean in to what God is trying to tell you.
Lean in to what God wants to produce in you for the next season of your life.

Don't Confuse Resistance with Redirection

Listen to me, opposition doesn't always mean "no."

It might mean "*you're in the right place, push anyway.*"

If God called you to it, then this season has purpose in it, even if you don't understand it right now. I can assure you losing some giants in my family last year and experiencing what I was experiencing with my grandmother rocked me to my core and again questioned my call and my assignment. It wasn't looking like I thought it was supposed to look like. It wasn't feeling like I thought it'd feel like when you give God your yes. But again, everything we face, everything we go through is positioning us, is marinating us for the next.

I had to learn how to forgive at an entirely different level.

I had to forgive quickly when I didn't understand.

I had to learn how to communicate differently.

I know Gramps gained her wings and to be honest, I'm so glad she did. I'm so glad she was able to leave this earth and not have to suffer anymore.

Now she wasn't always nice, she was a feisty thing from the very first memory of her. Yet I did not doubt she loved me in her own way and that she was proud of who I had become. And I know she felt my love for her as she was deteriorating and I'd do it all over again to make sure she knew she was loved and appreciated in her final days. So no, this chapter may not feel inspirational. But it's *essential.*

Because growth doesn't happen in the spotlight.

It happens in the dark.

When you're uncomfortable.

When you're stretching.

When you're choosing to believe what He said even when nothing around you looks like it.

It's in the hard times you learn not to retreat, not to run and hide, but stand and listen. Stand and fight. Stand and guard. Stand and watch.

Do you think the enemy cares about anything you love? That he and his army of imps care about anything you value? Every time you tuck your tail, run and hide the enemy wins. Scripture tells us that in every single battle, when the leaders were obedient, they won. Not some times, but EVERY SINGLE TIME.

Can you lean in and hear God during the hardest times of your life?

Can you lean in and hear God when the one you love dearly is being mistreated and you can't do anything about it?

Can you lean in and hear God when you're losing family member after family member and having a hard time navigating what life looks like without them?

It's in the pressures of life where the best of the best is produced.

And guess what?
That's where the oil is made.
That's where the diamonds are made.
Not in applause. But in pressure.
You're still on the right path.
So keep going.

My Life Poured Out

Affirmations

Hard times don't cancel my calling.
I trust God even when I don't understand the process.
I'm not alone, He walks with me.
I am being refined, not rejected.
I believe there is purpose in this pressure.
This season is stretching me for the next one.
I'll keep going, even now.

Midwife Moment

Now it's your turn to push, to breathe, to birth something from within.

1. What part of your life feels the hardest right now? *Name it. Don't gloss over it. Be honest about what's weighing you down.*
2. What has God already spoken over your life that this hard season is trying to make you forget? *Write down the truth. Put it up somewhere visible. Speak it daily.*
3. How has pain revealed parts of your purpose you weren't aware of before?
4. What gift, calling, or strength have you discovered in the middle of your pressure?

Journal Prompt:

"Even though this hurts, I still believe..."

Now finish that sentence in your own words. Don't hold back.

Girl, Release that ...ish

> "Forgiveness isn't a free pass, it's a holy release. You're not letting them off the hook. You're getting off the hook yourself."
>
> - Temeka Thompson

Chapter 4

Before you go any further, I want you to pause. Sit in these past few chapters where I've bled before you.

Like I say on my podcast. Grab your water, grab your wine, or your favorite drink. Then breathe in... and exhale.

Remember, you're reading this book because somewhere in your life you've been hiding, you've been afraid and you've felt unworthy.

You've wondered if God made a mistake when He called you. You thought you had to be perfect. And some of you have been so wounded by the church, or the saints, you can't even imagine God still seeing you.

I pray that as you've walked through these pages, you've started to see through the fog of those lies and realize you are still chosen.

This chapter is going to cost you something. It cost me.

Not because I had to dig deep to write it, but because every day I have to dig deep to live it, and you'll have to do the same. Every day is a new opportunity for you to choose God.

This is the ***"unclog the well" chapter,*** the part of your journey where obedience can't flow freely until the heart is cleared of what's been clogging it: unforgiveness, resentment, shame, and buried grief.

And let me be real with you, ***forgiveness is not for the faint of heart.***

And while everyone is capable of forgiving, everyone isn't willing to do the hard work to do it. It's not a one time prayer or a pretty phrase we throw around at Bible study. It's not a performance—it's a process, it's a journey. Forgiveness is absolutely a decision.

A bloody, soul-wrestling, throat-closing, pride-dismantling decision to let go of the debt someone owes you, the pain you carry that you have now idolized and made a home in. The anger that rises from the depths of your belly when you think about what they did to you, what they said to you, how they made you feel, how they didn't consider you, how they were selfish, how they had the audacity to disrespect you, how they treated your family member like they weren't worth being born. When you think about it or them, you see red, you feel anger, you feel bitterness it aches in your bones. I think we can all think of one situation or one person where this is real in our life now or in the past.

And if I'm being completely honest, I didn't want to let go. Because being the victim is easy. It's easy to blame others. There is no responsibility in that role, no accountability. No need to wrestle with compassion, understanding, surrender, maturity, empathy or unconditional love. The kind of love that covers a multitude of sins. As much as I wanted to love my father, I didn't want to forgive him for not being there. The two couldn't co-exist together. I didn't want to forgive the people who violated my body and my trust. I didn't want to forgive the versions of me that betrayed myself to be loved, to be seen.

And I definitely didn't want to admit that, on some level I needed to forgive God. Not because he wasn't good. But because of the expectation that I had of Him to save, love, and rescue me in many areas of my life. I didn't see His hands covering me as clearly as I do now. Through my pain of disappointment, I grew bitter with Him.

I doubted He could do the impossible because of what I endured, nor realizing it's because of His grace, His mercy, His love, His protection that I'm even able to write this book today. In my selfishness, I grew angry with God because my mother died. I prayed and prayed and expected for Him to heal her here on this side of the dirt, and I was so angry yet too embarrassed and prideful to admit I was angry, because I did love God.

I just didn't understand why He would take someone I cherished the most away from me in the prime of my young adult life where I felt I needed her the most. I didn't know how to be a wife or a mother and I really needed her to navigate this new space. I wasn't ready and I grew bitter, I was so angry. After all, I was His child, she was His child, we believed and because of that, I expected him to come through and when it didn't happen...words can't describe the level of pain, hurt, anger, rage, and bitterness that started to form inside of me.

I had to learn that letting go doesn't mean forgetting what someone else has or hasn't done. It doesn't mean that I pretend that it doesn't hurt, no it hurts, and it hurts like hell. It means that I decide when the pain no longer gets to run my life.

The pain of the disappointment, the pain of the betrayal, the pain no longer gets to hijack my emotions, the pain no longer gets to dictate how I show up in a room or how I love someone or treat someone. The pain now gets a master to teach it how to respond, when to respond, how to pull back the layers, see it, address it, deal with it and carry on.

And I've had to do that work, over and over and over again. It really is a journey. I've had to forgive people I never thought I could. I've had to release offenses that shaped my entire identity.

I've had to look in the mirror and forgive the version of me who didn't know how to fight for me, how to love for me. And I'll tell you the hardest part, the hardest part was forgiving myself.

What Forgiveness Really Means

Let's break this down, because people get it twisted.

To forgive doesn't mean to forget.
To forgive doesn't mean you're weak.
To forgive doesn't mean what they did was okay.

It means you're choosing not to let what happened continue to have power over your mind, your heart, or your health.

Here's how I define it:

"***Forgiveness is giving up the right to hurt people for hurting you.***"

Whew. Let that sit and rest for just a minute.

Forgiveness is not letting someone off the hook, it's getting yourself off the hook. It's untying your soul from bitterness, from rage, and from internal captivity.

When we hold onto unforgiveness, we keep drinking poison expecting the other person to die. Not realizing, we're really the ones dying because they've more than likely moved on. When we release it, something shifts, not just spiritually, but physically.

How we live our lives and show up everyday is filtered through our unforgiveness subconsciously if we don't let it go. How we treat others, how we love others, how we communicate with others, those who really do care for us, and strangers. Unforgiveness is blinded by our desperation for revenge and it has no concept of a fair playing field. The longer we hold it, the more it impacts us emotionally, physically and spiritually.

How Forgiveness Impacts the Body and the Brain

Science backs up what the Bible already taught us, forgiveness heals. Here's what happens in your body when you choose to forgive:

- Your brain calms down.
- Studies show that when you forgive, the amygdala (the fear and anger center of your brain) becomes less active. Your prefrontal cortex—the rational, decision-making part takes over, helping you feel more peace and clarity.
- Your heart literally softens.
- Forgiveness has been linked to lower blood pressure, decreased heart rate, and better cardiovascular health.
- Your stress levels drop.
- When you release resentment, your body produces less cortisol (the stress hormone). Chronic stress is connected to weight gain, inflammation, and disease. Forgiveness literally lets your body breathe again.
- Your immune system strengthens.
- Long-term unforgiveness can weaken your immune response, making you more prone to illness. Forgiveness boosts immunity and helps regulate your nervous system.
- Your mental clarity returns.
- Resentment clutters the mind. Forgiveness clears it. People who practice forgiveness regularly report higher levels of emotional resilience, clarity, empathy, and joy.

So no, forgiveness isn't just a spiritual thing, *it's a form of physical healing*. It's how we partner with God in restoring the body, renewing the mind, and protecting the soul.

Now, I want to remind you we're only as juicy and flavorful as our marination process. And there's also a nation of women waiting for your full surrender.

Forgiveness with No Apology

I hear you sis. You're saying, "But you don't know what they did. You don't know how it impacted my life."

I had to forgive someone who never said sorry. Someone who may never say sorry. Someone who probably doesn't even think they did anything wrong.

Now that's hard.

It's one thing to forgive when restoration is on the table. But to forgive when the wound is still fresh? To release someone when it feels like they've moved on without accountability? That takes surrender. And I couldn't move forward and carry resentment at the same time.

So I laid it down.
Tears in my eyes.
Grief in my chest.
Anger still lingering.
I laid it down.

Forgiveness is giving up the right to hurt someone else, whether out of revenge or unresolved pain. And I choose to surrender my right to retaliate. I chose to honor God with my life over my emotions. Not because I felt like it, but because I was called to something bigger. And it wasn't easy.

I shared with you what happened in the last chapter about Gramps. The most recent challenge of forgiveness was with a close relative I grew up adoring who has been in my life all of my life. I wanted to be like her when I grew up. I'd been away from home for at least 10 or 12 years. It was too painful to show up and smile and be present when I missed my mother so much. My mother, she was the heartbeat of our family branch with her smile, her wisdom, her laugh. She was joy, she would light up the room. And after trying to keep the routine of making annual or bi-annual trips back to Florida, it became unbearable and life started evolving as my husband and I were building our own family and our own traditions. It was much easier to call or send cards and flowers back home.

My cousin gave my sister and I the nudge that we should probably get home more as my grandmother was getting older. It didn't really hit until I'd sent Gramps some flowers for Mother's Day, called shortly after I received the delivery notification and she said she didn't get the flowers. I called her sister to have her double check and she didn't see the flowers, and I asked my uncle and he didn't see the flowers. So I called the flower company to figure out what happened. They sent another delivery out free of charge the next day. Three days later, my aunt found the flowers from the first delivery, still in the box, in Gramps bedroom. It was then I knew her brain was starting to betray her and I needed to get back home.

It was almost like being in a time capsule stepping back into Gramps' house. The same paint on the walls since I was a little girl, the same carpet, dust choking the air out of the atmosphere, the white curtains that used to be crisp and clean now hang as a dingy, beige cloth that now prevents the light from shining in bright through the blinds of the windows that seemed to now always remain closed.

The same couches that sucked you in when you sat down to the newly bolted door to keep Gramps from what seemed like escaping. And the now fragile, frail, gentle, slow moving Gramps. I'd never seen my grandmother like this before. She was feisty, she was a mover and a shaker and her love language was fussing. I couldn't sit in the moment long because I had to navigate the space for my daughter who was a teenager now and hadn't seen her great grandmother since she was 8 years old.

As nostalgic as the moment was re-entering the house, reality had to set in very quickly. I realized I missed out on many years. Now Gramps and I didn't have the relationships you see on the Disney channel or that you might've read about in the fairy tales. But she was my grandmother, she helped my mother raise us and I believe she gave us her last many of days. So now it was my turn. I couldn't help but think, "Why didn't my aunt or uncle say anything sooner?"

Because she was still feisty and still laughing, I knew we had some time left so I made a decision to enjoy it. I asked important questions about her health, estate planning, etc. ACCESS DENIED. I didn't understand. It wasn't like I was coming after my Gramps' estate, it wasn't like I was trying to take over, I genuinely cared and wanted to know. And because my husband and I finished our estate planning a few years ago, I was excited about having the conversation. Because my mother didn't have that conversation with us and she didn't have life insurance when she died and to this day I have no idea who took care of the cost of everything. It was all a blur. So I thought this was a responsible, adult, mature conversation to have with family, but with each question we were denied access.

I couldn't help thinking, "What are you trying to hide?" We should be okay with having a normal conversation about estate planning. The family should know what's going on, what's being inherited, there should be an estate that's clear. And we all should be able to bring some type of value or consideration to the table. Nope.

My hat goes off to every caregiver, the weight of caregiving is a lot. I offered to give the family a week or two off so they could take a break. I was told, "No, you don't have to do that, live your life."

I asked every health care worker questions, not just to gather facts, but to protect Gramps and another aunt living in the home. I remember having a conversation with my grandmother and trying to find out what she'd like to do. She was still a human being no matter how her brain was starting to cheat her of her precious life. She still had life in her and I wanted to share some last memories with her. I found out she hadn't ever been to the beach. Something I never realized. Lived in Florida all of her life and had never been to the beach. My daughter couldn't believe it and it was such a precious moment that I was able to share with her how segregation really impacted the lives of black families. As a child my grandmother, our family, people of color weren't allowed on the beach. So they swam and had fun at lakes as children. Then when she started working, she worked until she retired and the time off she did take, it was often at home to watch my sister and I.

When I took her to Panama City Beach she was captivated by the trees. She had her pearls on and she was cute, cute honey!!! Once we got to the beach, her walking cane in tow, she walked out across the sand, looked at the water, she talked to strangers and we ran into this one lady who blessed my entire soul. She was so kind with Gramps, she talked with her as long as Gramps entertained her, we took photos, she laughed and then she got hot and hungry and was ready to go. Now if you know anything about a woman when they get hot and hungry, you better figure something out fast. We went to Waffle House afterwards, and she was so excited to eat. I asked her what she wanted to eat. She asked, "Oh, I can order?" "Yes Gramps," was my response. "You can have whatever you want." Her eyes lit up like a kid that was given an all-access pass to a desert buffet. It was such a sweet yet bitter moment. She ate until her heart was content. I had to hold back the tears on the way back to her house because all I could think about was, this might be her last great meal until my next visit.

I told you what her daily diet consisted of in the last chapter and I swear every time I saw her she was getting skinnier and more frail. I'm a fan of supplements, I'm a fan of organic foods, and alternative medicine (you know my relationship with my doctor, LOL),but I'm not a fan of neglect, and if something doesn't work, it's time to change course. Eating organic doesn't mean starvation.

And the way she was being talked to and shoved around. I just don't understand how you can treat your mother, your loved one, or another human being this way at this stage in their lives. The most fragile, tender stages of their lives when they can no longer take care of themselves. The cycle of life, they birth you, take care of you, raise you, you live your life, and when they can no longer do for themselves, the child then takes care of the parent(s). What did she do that made you so bitter that you can't love on her during this stage of life? She wasn't perfect, but she's still your mother.

When I was home I made sure they were fed and loved and I would send some things when I couldn't make it home. The more I visited, I could see things slipping through the cracks. The more she lost weight, the angrier I got. I started noticing a new caregiver each time I'd go home. I'm not paying for the caregiver so I realize consent isn't required, but it would've been great to have a conversation about it. I want to know what happened to the last one and who is this new one? I asked about installing cameras in the house that I'd pay for so we could have access while the workers were in the house during the day. Again. Access denied.

Now with every visit, I feel like I'm interviewing the caregivers to get to know them, to understand their temperament, to see if they actually have a love for this or if this was just a paycheck. There was one who truly had a love for it and it showed in every way.

I'm pretty sure it was the text message that Gramps had fallen and was in a coma in ICU that took me straight to bitterness; this could've been prevented. I realize there's a lot going in a moment like that, but a text message?

You know how it looks when you're in the eye of the storm and you have all these things going around you, you can see them, yet time stands still. I had that experience only two other times in my life, when I got the call from the hospital that my mother died and when the plane hit the pentagon during 9/11 while my son and I were in the building.

Unforgiveness was slowly creeping in, I think it actually rooted that day. The anger, the disappointment, the betrayal of information, the constant control, the neglect, the narcissistic behavior, it was literally a tornado of emotions that consumed me that day. The more I tried to ignore it, the more it swallowed me up.

In her final days, I believe Gramps felt loved. When she was in a coma, unresponsive; my sister and I ushered in God's presence into the hospital room.

We sang.
We prayed.
We worshipped. We played worship music.

And for a brief moment, she responded.
Her body moved.
Her eyes opened just enough to let us know she knew we were there.

After she transitioned a few weeks later, I was so relieved that she was finally in the BEST hands, the BEST care and her struggle here on earth was over.

Deaths and funerals sometimes bring out the best or the very worst of you. And it didn't get better. Control was the dominating force here. We were asked to be in place within 24 to 48 hours after Gramps passed. But once we arrived, we weren't invited to be a part of the planning, or any of the final decisions. Wait, we're her only living, blood grandchildren. I missed my daughter's award ceremonies of her freshmen year, something I can never get back. Another wound being opened. Rejection runs deep.

Now, I can't allow anyone to villanize my family or give you permission to continue to do the same for anyone else in your life. When people say and do things that trigger us, we have to take a step back and ask ourselves, "why does that hurt so deep? Why does this bother me so much? Why do I want to respond or retaliate with so much anger? Why do I feel like this?"

Another relative intervened and we were able to be a part of the planning of the service. But more unfolded and I know I told you in the last chapter it would take an entire book to talk about the funeral details. I promise I won't tell it all, I want to paint a picture so you can see that you may never get an apology and you can still forgive.

When someone transitions, they aren't the best looking. And the very last image of Gramps before she was taken was something I was told didn't remotely look like her, so I passed on seeing the final viewing because I didn't want to remember her that way (the coma was bad enough). During the wake, the funeral home had done an amazing job with her and her siblings said she looked really good. There was still time to see her based on the details listed in the newspaper, so I went over and again DENIED ACCESS. That's when unforgiveness got embedded. The relative with all the power had slipped away, saw her and made the final decision to close the casket although it had been published it would be open for public viewing. When I called her to find out why and ask her to open it, again I was DENIED ACCESS and hung up on.

So Sis, I get it. I was mad as HELL, I mean big mad. I heard and saw nothing but red for about two hours.

As the day settled, I also heard God whisper, "The assignment doesn't stop."

At that very moment, I couldn't lie, I felt like, "God miss me with that." I had to worship the morning of the funeral, so I could honor Gramps in the way she deserved. And another family member told me before I left Florida that weekend, "Now baby, don't allow this to keep you away from home." I told ya'll I was a runner.

I wanted to grieve in silence.
I wanted to grieve in rage.
I wanted to quit everything.
But God called me to pour anyway.
To forgive anyway.
To heal anyway.
To move anyway.
And everyday I push myself.

There is something powerful about a decision. One day, I woke up and I made a decision. I refused to allow bitterness and unforgiveness to put a rift in our family. There are too many families where siblings or aunts and other relatives aren't talking to each other. I decided that won't be me. It's not easy, every day I have to make the decision. Every time I go home, I have to make that decision. And that's without an apology. Because they don't think they did anything wrong. So even if you don't get an apology, you still get to choose forgiveness.

I know you might be thinking.
"That's too fast."
"That's not fair."
"She doesn't deserve it."
"They should pay."

I thought about all of that, too.

And here's what I've learned, forgiveness is not about fairness. It's about freedom. My freedom, not theirs.

Your freedom , not theirs.

Before you throw this book or close it and never finish it at this point, I want you to think about this. If I didn't forgive quickly, the bitterness would've taken over. And when God is calling you to serve, to lead, to pour, there's no room for clogged wells.

Unforgiveness is spiritual blockage. You can't flow when you're festering. You can't minister while marinating in misery. Or at least you shouldn't.

Think about this for just a minute. Jesus knew who Judas was long before Judas ever kissed His cheek in betrayal. He knew the lies, the greed, the deception, and the plan that would lead to His arrest. Yet, He still chose him. He still called him "friend." He still let him sit at the table. And not just that, He put Judas in charge of the money.

Jesus forgave Judas before Judas ever betrayed Him. Because forgiveness was never about the apology. It was about obedience.

Jesus showed us that forgiveness isn't for the one who hurt you, it's for the freedom that's waiting on the other side of your yes. Sometimes, the person who betrayed you will never apologize. They may never acknowledge the pain they caused. But you can still release them. You can still choose peace.

Forgiving without an apology doesn't make you foolish, it makes you free. If Jesus could extend grace knowing the cross was on the other side of Judas' betrayal, then maybe forgiveness for you isn't about keeping them close...it's about keeping your heart clean.

Because when you forgive without an apology, you stop waiting for closure from man and start walking in healing from God.

So I released it. Now I want to be 100% honest with you, I took some months of separation. I needed space. But I didn't stay long. I had to trust that God would handle what I couldn't. And I got back to the assignment, with tears, with a heavy heart from grieving, but with obedience.

Forgiving My Father

When I made the decision to forgive my father, God started to redeem the time for us. We have a good relationship now and I've finally reached the point where I've removed the expectations. I see and love my father for who he is. A smart, ambitious man with incredible drive. Flawed yes, but so am I.

Because I made the decision, I gained a better insight of his childhood, what he endured. He's been on his own since he was 15 years old and had no concept of being a good father in the landscape of his life. He had a dream he was chasing and it didn't involve children at the time. I didn't want my kids to grow up not knowing my father or his side of the family due to my unforgiveness. I chose not to be the carrier of generational unforgiveness. Did

I endure a lot as a child, yes. Did I blame my father, yes. I do believe had my father been in my life as a child, there were some things I would have never experienced or encountered. But if God allowed it, then it was for me to endure it. And because I endured it, there's nothing I can do about the past.

So I made a decision, and that decision brought healing and restoration to the both of us. I've been able to meet so many great family members that I wouldn't have been able to meet had I held onto the feeling of being discarded. Uncles, aunts, cousins, would I have loved to have them in my life as a child? Yes. But I choose to embrace this season and I'm grateful that I get to break a generational cycle so my kids can grow up knowing my paternal side of the family. Here's why that's important. I didn't know my mother's father's side of the family until he was on his death bed. Gramps didn't talk much about her father's side of the family. I had to ask other relatives about him and although he was killed while she was young, I don't remember his family being around and we had countless family gatherings.

My son was about five years old and started asking about his grandparents. We were away from all of our family in Florida, my mother had passed away a few years prior, my father wasn't in my life and Eric's mom was in Florida and at the time he didn't have a relationship with his father. So this was generations of separation with fathers. I was walking through my own healing journey through the grief of my mother and I was also tired of carrying the dead weight of my past.

I was at a church where the Co-Pastor was also a licensed Therapist. We had one session and she gave me an assignment to write a letter to my father. I didn't have to send the letter, I only needed to write it. So I wrote the letter and placed it in an envelope and held onto it for a while. I knew in order to stop the generational cycles of father's not being present I had to heal and then build a relationship with my father.

I think people underestimate the weight of the generational cycle breaker. Not only do we have to heal, but then we have to go and break the cycle so it doesn't affect the next generation most of the time without a guide.

I got the courage to mail the letter. My father was in the hospital when he actually read the letter and that opened up a bridge for us to talk. Talking led to more talking. He was so excited about my son and was proud of all of my accomplishments. Over the years, we grew to know each other more. There were still some setbacks because I was still expecting him to be the father I wanted him to be as a little girl and that wasn't possible for two reasons. 1. I wasn't a little girl anymore. 2. He wasn't that person. I never gave up on the restoration process. Through prayer, giving up my expectations, choosing to forgive daily and not giving up on the process, our relationship has been restored and I'm so grateful for our relationship now. I love him so much and I thank God for redeeming the time.

Some years ago, I remember attending a women's conference and the visiting Pastor gave us a forgiveness exercise. I wish I could find all the copious notes I took during his session, but I can't.

Here's what I remember. He told us to close our eyes and think about the people we needed to forgive. The ones that hurt us, the ones that disappointed us, the ones that violated us. As we thought about the situation, if a person's name or face appeared, we still needed to forgive them. As I thought about this, my dad showed up again and I was a little confused because I was starting the process, things were going pretty good. While in motion, I was still a little disappointed he wasn't in my life as a child. Wondering if I would've been molested if he was present, if I would've married the man I married if he was present. Now Eric is a keeper, we're lifers at this point, but these are things you question when you don't know. On that day I made the decision not to hold my father captive for those things I couldn't answer or that he couldn't answer either.

God has redeemed and restored my relationship with my father. I remember driving down I-295 in DC and hitting a yellow barrel on the highway in Eric's brand new Chevy Tahoe. I was scared to tell Eric I'd just kissed a caution barrel with his brand new truck and the barrel left a permanent imprint to remind me it almost won the street race - because he idolizes his vehicles. What did I do? I called my dad and he reassured me that Eric was more concerned about me than the vehicle. Now I know that was my dad reassuring me and also speaking it into the atmosphere so he wouldn't have to hurt Eric for thinking otherwise, LOL.

And the time when I walked away from a job for my next job opportunity only to be devastated when they withdrew their offer two days before I was scheduled to start and I was without a job. I have been working since I was 15 years old. I was making double Eric's income and I wasn't sure how ends were going to meet. I remember my dad telling me not to worry. Asking me what we needed to at least close the gap and for two years, he supplemented my income so our house didn't fall apart. And he kept reassuring me that God has something greater for me.

And when Eric and I were on the brink of divorce there were some phone calls I'd make to my dad and he'd reassure me, "Baby girl, what you and Eric have is a good thing, challenges come and go and you don't want to lose a good thing over something that won't matter in a couple of years." He was fathering. Then there's the first Christmas he actually came and stayed with me and my family. Although I was in my late 30s, it was such a great Christmas not because of the gifts, but because I was spending it with my dad. I've met his brothers and sisters and developed great relationships with them and so have my kids. I've learned so much about him and his family through the years and after talking with one of his sisters, I now know that he was living and doing all that he knew how to do.

Again, my father was on his own around the age of 15 trying to navigate life and survive from an abusive situation with his step-father and was caught up in a child custody battle between his parents. Then moving into a home with other family members, he was trying to figure out where and how he fit in life. Not feeling accepted he navigated his own way. Served in the army during Vietnam, got out then had a life changing experience where he was shot by Detroit police officers and declared dead on the scene and then God brought him back to life.

It's about perspective. And how life serves people has an impact on how they show up in life and for other people. Their hurts, their pains, their trials, how they're loved or not loved, all impact how they show up in life. I didn't understand that as a child. This isn't an excuse for my father not being there as a child, it's about letting go. There's nothing we can do about the past. We can't go back and reshape history. All we can do is determine how we show up in the present and in the future. And we've decided we're going to show up for each other unapologetically.

I've decided to love him for who he is and he is amazing. When you release the anger you get to enjoy life more. I've learned so much about my father in these past ten years that makes me love him more and allows me to extend grace. As a little girl I only knew one uncle, my mom's brother, and all of my mother's uncles. Although they were my great uncles, I called them uncle because we were all so close. Now I have four uncles on my dad's side, three more uncles on my mom's side (from her father) and three aunts and cousins galore on my dad's side. The relationships we've built have been one for a Disney movie.

You could be the very one selected to break a generational cycle, but pride, shame, and unforgiveness has you in a choke hold. It was easy for me to pass down hate to my kids about my father, but I chose not to do that. I chose for them to develop their own relationship with their grandfather. The only thing I asked my dad to do was never promise them anything. And to this very moment, he has honored my request. He'll make sure they have the best, he'll show up for their graduations and reach out on birthdays. He has really done a great job at showing up in life for his family and that means so much.

You are responsible for what you pass down to the next generation. Will you pass along hate, will you pass along division, will you pass along resentment, will you pass it on? Don't be the family where sisters and brothers won't talk to each other, the family that fights at their parent's funerals and who hate to breathe in the same airspace. You are responsible for the hate you give and the hate you pass along and God is going to hold you accountable. Know that until you let it go of your ish, obedience can't fully flow through you. I'm not saying you can't have your boundaries, but remember you don't need an apology to let it go.

For years, I carried silent wounds. Maybe not so silent in this season. My anger resounded loudly through my insecurities, through my pain, through my desire to be loved as I was. Not because of my smile, not because I was cute, not because of my body, but because I was Temeka.

Not all of them were loud or dramatic. Some were quiet absences, calls not made, moments missed, protection never offered. I grew up learning how to protect myself because I didn't feel safe to lean on what should've been safe. You have to remember everything I thought was safe, turned out not being safe at all.

The older I got, I thought I had moved on. Even when I got married, I thought I had moved on. But every time when Eric let me down... every time I doubted my worth, every time I needed to be in control, I was bleeding from the unhealed place of a daughter who for the first half of her life never heard, *"I'm proud of you. I love you. I see you."* And having her father show up for her.

Forgiveness didn't start with a phone call. It started with a funeral. I had to bury the version of my father I wished I had, so I could accept the reality of who he is, and release him.

While he did apologize right away (because he did), I didn't let go because he apologized. I let go because I chose to. *Because I was ready to live.*

Forgiveness is a choice and every day you have to make that choice.

Forgiving Those Who Violated Me

My dad's name wasn't the only name that popped up at that woman's conference. Every person who violated me did.

There were a few things holding me back. One of the biggest choke holds preventing me from writing this book was that I wanted to make sure I still honored my family while telling my story and I didn't want to be judged and I didn't want to set my family back with guilt, shame or blame.

There are no soft words for this. Being violated changes something in you. It twists your sense of safety. It builds walls where innocence used to live. And for a long time, I didn't know how to talk about what happened. I held onto pain like a badge, proof of how strong I was. Proof I had a reason to be angry. But strength built on pain isn't the same as freedom.

Being violated is like a thief coming to steal every trace of innocence and purity you have only to find out the thief is someone you know. Someone you once trusted.

To say I was confused doesn't even give justice to the betrayal of having to protect yourself from a loved one. Not really knowing who or what to trust.

How they look at you. The disgusted gleam of demons dancing behind glassed over eyes as they undress you. As they manipulate you. As they twist your thoughts, your feelings, and silence your voice before you even realize you had one.

And because there's no lifeline in sight, you learn how to float in pain.

You learn how to survive in silence, in darkness, in the shards of crumbled glass.

Then, as it continues for years, what once hurt you tricks your mind into believing it's easier to accept it than fight it. You convince yourself to find some type of control, some type of dignity in the middle of what's already been undone. But you can't piece together what's already shattered.

The disgust. The shame. The anger. The years I spent hating my own body. For the first time, I felt unworthy without even understanding the language to know what that meant. The frustration of not being able to fix what I didn't break.

Sis, breathe.

I've come to save you.
I've come to make space for you in this moment.
It wasn't your fault.
It was NEVER your fault.

And because we survived it, we can break free.

Here's the thing about survival, when you're trying to protect what's left of you, you start doing whatever it takes to keep from breaking completely.

As it continued, I didn't understand why I was always the target. At the same time, I knew I had to protect my younger sister. So I succumbed to the abuse because I was afraid that if I didn't, they would target her. We were the only girls around most of the time, my mother worked two and three jobs, and while Gramps worked one, it seemed like most of the time there were no adults around.

At some point, the violation shifted.

It went from "*What is happening?*"
To "*are we supposed to be doing this?*"
To "*wait...stop...that hurts...NO.*"

And then, somehow, it started to feel good—and I desired it.

This experience shaped how I sought out relationships as a teenager, seeking sex. I should've been concerned about cheer practice, my grades, and high school parties. Instead it was survival.

Then after being raped by a family member, I got angry.

I remember telling my mother and I think she was trying to process it at first. It was a delicate situation because we were living in the relative's home; which meant if she confronted them, we'd probably have to find another place to live. So I felt bad for even placing my mother in that situation knowing how hard it was for her to keep us in a clean, safe and affordable environment. I'm not sure if she had the conversation or not (it was something we never discussed again), but as a child I felt like she didn't believe me. To this day, I don't know if it was because she dealt with the same as a child or if she didn't know how to handle the situation. After that, I felt mute and realized I needed to protect myself, so I learned the art of manipulation with my body and used it to benefit me. I can size a dude up a mile away. A protection mechanism I learned until I realized I could save myself.

Forgiveness isn't about saying "*It's okay.*"

Because it wasn't okay.

I had to release it so it wouldn't rot inside me.

I had to hand God the shattered pieces and say, "*Here. I can't carry this anymore. I'm ready to heal, even if they never apologize.*"

Forgiving Myself

If I'm being completely honest, forgiving myself was the hardest part. I could extend grace to others and still crucify myself.

Every poor decision.
Every moment I ignored the red flags.
Every time I stayed too long, settled too small, or silenced my voice, I held it against myself.

It didn't matter what I accomplished, it didn't matter how I was being celebrated, the self sabotage yelled louder. I could hear my mother in my ear, "You have no common sense." That was the theme of my life growing up. I was book smart with no common sense. "You're just like your father." And to only know how he wasn't showing up didn't make me feel good. I now take it as a compliment, he and I are a lot alike in many ways. The Kyler blood runs strong.

I didn't think anything could quiet the noise in my head constantly reminding me that I wasn't enough. Constantly recounting what others had spoken over my life, the beliefs of what I thought I was because I allowed others to dictate the narrative over my life. Thinking about suicide wasn't just a thought and even after attempting, I beat myself up about it because I couldn't even do that right.

Oh how I beat myself up because I didn't know how to love me. I didn't know my value, I didn't know my purpose. I didn't know where to begin. I felt so off track and at one point in my life the road was so dusty as I stood in the distance of what seemed to be too far for me to get back on track. Nothingness was a full being for me. I was numb to what life had to offer, suffocating with each breath I breathed.

I was a full adult, active in the church, singing on the praise and worship team and suffocating. Looking at the people around me thinking I'd never be holy enough. I was too damaged, I was too mean.

God can't do anything with my fragments. I can't pray like they pray, I can't shout like they shout, I can't dance like they dance, I don't know the word of God like they know the word of God.

I thought everybody else was perfect, because "Holiness was the standard". I couldn't dress it up and meet the standard, I couldn't sing it up and meet the standard, I couldn't pray enough to meet the standard, I couldn't shout enough to meet the standard.

So at every breath I took, I was suffocating, losing hope, losing life, losing a sense of belonging, losing a sense of worth.

Then God whispered, "*If I've already forgiven you, why are you still punishing yourself?*"

The whisper got louder and I realized God was talking to me. That whisper of hope embraced me as if it was a genie coming from the lamp or the twirl from Cinderella's fairy godmother's magic wand.

I didn't know it then, but I know now it was the *Holy Spirit.* It breathed life into me that day. It held me that day. It showed me I was loved that day, that I was enough that day. The Holy Spirit saved my life that day.

And in case you're in an empty place, let this be the whisper that saves your life.

The whisper that says, you're worthy of life. You are enough. You are wonderfully and fearfully made. There is now no condemnation for those who love the Lord, for those who are called according to His purpose.

And Sis, you're called to His purpose. You are purpose. Your very existence here means there is more. And I need you to survive. I need you to heal, I need you to move in all that God has purposed for your life. You are not a mistake.

I had to look in the mirror and say, "*I forgive you. You did the best you could with what you knew at the time. But now, we're moving forward, not in guilt, not in shame, in grace.*"

The more I rehearsed this, the more I started to believe it. When I finally got it, there was no turning back.

Do the whispers try to creep back up? Yes they do, the difference between before the encounter with the holy spirit and now is that now I have a reassurance. God has shown me too much, done too much, kept me from too much and confirmed too much for me to believe the lie. I now have an arsenal to fight back the lies. The word of God and the power of my testimony.

Forgiving God

And yes, I had to forgive God, too.

Because I was carrying disappointment I never named. As much as I loved God, I was mad He didn't heal my mother here on earth.

I was mad He allowed her to die. I was mad He allowed the molestation to last as long as it did and he didn't stop it.

That He didn't shield me. That He didn't intervene in the ways I thought He should've.

Mad He didn't bring my father into my life sooner.

Mad my son was misbehaving.

Mad my son was molested by a family member (*we were supposed to be breaking the cycle God*). And I did everything I knew to protect him. I knew what to look for. It blind sided me.

Mad I was in a military career that I hated for a long time.

Mad I was in a life I hated.

Mad I was in a marriage I hated for some time.

Just mad.

It felt wrong for me to even say it out loud. But God can handle your honesty. He'd rather you bring Him your pain than pretend it doesn't exist.

I had to open my heart and say, "God, I'm hurt. But I still trust You. Help my unbelief. Heal my anger. Hold me through it." And He did.

I had to get to my lowest level, at the feet of Jesus and prepare an altar and lay every burden down. Every fear, every pain, every disappointment, every anger, every resentment, the bitterness and just lay it there and surrender, empty myself out with all sincerity. My heart surrendered, my life surrendered, my body surrendered, my mind surrendered, my soul surrendered and repent.

Admitting the Wound

One of the first steps in recovering from any addiction, whether to substance abuse, trauma, people, or pain, it's admitting there's a problem.

And I had one.

I was addicted to unforgiveness.

I wore my wounds like a badge of honor and covered them with a cape of strength.

I smiled. I showed up. I prayed hard. I poured out.

Underneath it all, I was bleeding. Quietly. Constantly.

I called it resilience.

If I'm being honest, it was residue.

I thought I had moved on. I thought time had healed what I refused to confront. But pain doesn't expire because we bury it.

Unforgiveness doesn't just live in your thoughts, it lives in your body.

In your reactions.
In your silence.
In your inability to fully trust, love or rest.

And I couldn't heal what I was still holding on to. Hear me, God couldn't heal what I was still holding on to or who I was pretending to be. So I had to tell the truth to God and myself, "I'm still holding this."

That admission was the beginning of my healing.

Because healing doesn't start with a sermon or a journal entry.

It starts with confession. It starts with a decision.
It starts when you admit what they did still hurts.
That what you lost still matters.
That you're not as over it as you pretend to be.

And that's not weakness.
That's honesty.
That's where God meets us.

So if you've been carrying something for years, anger, grief, betrayal, shame. I want to invite you to do the bravest thing: **admit it, and make the decision to forgive.**

You don't have to solve it today.
You don't have to have all the answers or even all of the details or know how to make it right.
But you do have to be honest.
That's where healing begins.

Obedience > Perfection

I didn't do it perfectly.

I still had questions.

I still cried.

And I was even still angry.

But I chose obedience.

This is what Obedience Over Perfection looks like in real time.

Choosing to pour when you feel empty.
Choosing to heal while you're still hurting.
Choosing to forgive when no apology was offered.
Choosing to walk in purpose when the wound is still fresh.

So if you're reading this and battling whether or not to let go...

Whether or not to forgive...
Whether or not you're ready to move forward...
Let this be your gentle nudge
It's not about perfection.
It's about obedience.

And obedience doesn't wait for perfect conditions.

It just says yes even when the heart still stings.

My Life Poured Out

Affirmations

I am not what happened to me.
I release the pain I was never created to carry.
I forgive others, not because they earned it, but because I'm choosing freedom.
I forgive myself for surviving in ways that no longer serve me.
I release resentment. I release guilt. I release the need for revenge.
I trust God with my healing, and I walk forward whole.

Midwife Moment

Now it's your turn to push, to breathe, to birth something from within.

1. Who are you still carrying in your spirit?

List their names. Write what they did. Now say aloud: "*I release them. I forgive. I choose freedom.*"

2. What are you still holding against yourself?

Write a letter of grace to the younger you, from the healed version of you.

3. Be honest: Are you upset with God?

Don't filter your truth. Write it out. Then ask Him to meet you in that honesty, and listen for His response.

Midwife Moment

4. Declare this aloud:

"This pain ends with me. This bitterness ends with me. I forgive, and I am free."

Hey Sis, that was a hard chapter and if you made it here, I know you need a moment to just breathe. I want to encourage you, scan the QR code below and check out this video.

You are the Assignment

> My life wasn't poured out for applause. It was poured out for the assignment.

\- Temeka Thompson

Chapter 5

Sis, you've made it this far through the healing, the reflection, the hard truths, and the heart work. That alone deserves to be celebrated. You didn't quit. You didn't shrink back. You've allowed God to peel back layers, confront lies, and begin restoring what life tried to bury and I'm so proud of you.

Before you keep reading, pause.
Breathe in grace.
Exhale fear.

And whisper this to yourself, "I'm still here. I'm still chosen. I'm still becoming."

This is the chapter where you become still enough to see yourself. This is where your "becoming" meets your "doing." Where your healing turns into a movement.

Where your yes becomes a weapon.

Who Are You Still Carrying?

I'm going to ask you a super honest but very important question.

Have you released the person you've been carrying in your spirit?

Why am I asking this at the top of the chapter? Because it's essential as we move forward.

There's something about you that cannot be duplicated. But if you're still carrying someone else in your spirit, their expectations, their rejection, their opinion of you, you'll miss what God placed uniquely inside of you every single time.

And here's the truth: the enemy has been hoping you'd never figure that out.

You're not just called.
You're not just gifted.
You are anointed.

You carry oil that can't be emulated and grace that didn't come from anything you did, it came from Heaven, tailor-made for you.

I get it. You've probably spent much of your life being compared, overlooked, underestimated, or trying so hard to be "enough" that shrinking became your safety net.

So you stopped showing up full out. You gravitated to rooms and groups where you could easily hide so you could protect yourself from being hurt again, protecting yourself from being a target for the wounded to destroy.

Here's what I want you to hear:
YOU ARE THE TABLE.
So stop looking for one.
You are the secret sauce.

And what God placed in you is not up for negotiation.

The Lie of Not Enough

There's a lie many of us have unknowingly chewed up and swallowed:
"I'm not enough."

It shows up subtly.

When you downplay your accomplishments in a room full of confident people.

When you second-guess every decision.

When you scroll social media and wonder if your version of beauty, business, or boldness is even valid.

When you mute yourself because someone once told you you were too loud, too strong, or too much.

But God whispered to me one day, right in the middle of my comparison:
"*They may do it well, but not like you. Because they don't carry what you carry.*"

You are not just one of many. You are the only one who can carry your calling the way you were designed to. That's what makes you irreplaceable.

Jeremiah 1:5 says, "*Before I formed you in your mother's womb, I knew you. I set you apart.*" That means your identity was established before insecurity ever had a voice.

Then there's Deborah, a woman who led nations, judged with wisdom, and went to war with courage. She didn't wait for a title. She operated in her genius, her authority, and her assignment. And male leaders sought her out and wouldn't go into battle without her. In a culture that silenced women, she led anyway. Did you hear me? In a male dominated era, the leaders of armies sought out a woman (Deborah) to lead them and wouldn't go into battle without her. I don't think we hear enough about Deborah across pulpits on Sunday mornings. She was a fierce and wise woman. And there was not ONE person on earth who carried what she carried. The same is true for you (insert your name).

And Mary, she carried the Savior of the world. She wasn't chosen because she was perfect; she was chosen because she said *yes*.

You're not less spiritual because you don't have a platform.

You're not less powerful because you're not behind a pulpit.

You're not less qualified because you don't have the right network or name.

Your yes is what makes you dangerous.

Your obedience is what opens heaven.

And your uniqueness? That's your superpower.

You Are Not Random

So no, you're not random. God didn't make you by accident. You are not an accident.

Maybe to your parents only because they didn't realize God had already preplanned you.

He didn't give you your laugh, your voice, your creativity, or your strength just for fun. Every detail was intentional, even the quirks that made you question yourself. The very hairs on your head are calculated.

Sis, this chapter is your permission slip to *become.*

To stop shrinking.
To stop dimming your light to make others comfortable.
To stop editing your essence to fit into rooms God never assigned you to, mic drop!

What makes you different is what makes you divine.

As my sister Sarah Jakes-Roberts says, *"It's time for you to get on your square, your block, because we need you."*

It's necessary.

The world doesn't need another carbon copy. It needs your authenticity, your scars, your wisdom, your sound.

Nothing is Wasted

Nothing is wasted when it's surrendered to God.

Purpose isn't waiting for you on the mountaintop.

It's not just in the next big win or the spotlight moment.

Purpose is found in the valley.
In the stretch.
In the silence.
In the moments nobody claps for.

We've been conditioned to look for purpose in the loud moments, the breakthroughs, the applause, the milestones. But what if purpose whispers? What if it shows up when you're washing dishes, questioning your worth? What if it hides in the seasons of invisibility, when no one sees you but God?

Sis, purpose isn't something you chase. It's something you uncover layer by layer, in obedience and surrender.

For years, I thought purpose needed a platform. I thought it had to be polished, branded, and clear. God showed me my most purpose-filled seasons didn't look like purpose at all.

They looked like *pressure.*
They looked like *pain.*
They looked like *process.*

I'm reminded of a song Fantasia sings, "*I am who I am today, because God used my mistakes. He worked them for my good, like no one else ever could. It was necessary*".

Purpose showed up in my breakdown before the breakthrough.

In the betrayal that forced me to set boundaries.

In the grief that drove me to the feet of Jesus.

In the stillness where I finally learned to hear His voice over everyone else's.

Purpose was in the very places I tried to escape from. When I finally stopped running, when I stopped trying to organize my calling into neat little boxes, I learned purpose was never a destination.

It was always process.

You my dear ARE PURPOSE

Joseph was sold, betrayed, imprisoned, and forgotten yet purpose never left him. Even in the dungeon, he was being prepared for the palace. What they meant for evil, God used for good.

And Jesus, even His crucifixion carried purpose. It didn't look like victory. It looked like defeat, suffering, and pain. But it was the greatest act of love and redemption the world has ever seen.

So if you're in a season that doesn't look like purpose, don't panic.

The heartbreak, the job loss, the quiet nights, the unanswered prayers, the parenting struggles, the loss of a loved one, the late night tears nobody sees, it's all being used.

There is no detour in the Kingdom.
No delay without development.
Nothing is wasted.
Not even this.

So stop asking "Why me?" and start asking "God, what are You revealing through this?"

Purpose isn't found by force.

It's found in presence in stillness in being, before building.

Even here, sis, you are purpose.

There comes a moment when healing isn't just about you

It's not just about you getting unstuck, breaking free from the past, or rediscovering your worth.

I'll never forget our son ran away from home twice when he was in middle school and ended up at church both times. He wasn't a bad child, just impulsive. He'd do things without thinking about the consequences, and he was cute and funny. Still, he didn't like to take accountability for his actions (we thank God for maturity and deliverance). And we were a family that believed in disciplining in a way where you learned life lessons. And he'd run from those consequences. Do you know how embarrassing it is for the youth leader's child to run away from home? He knew God at an early age and had encounters with God.

As much as we were terrified when he was gone, we were grateful that he knew enough to run to the house of refuge. But God used it. The most embarrassing, vulnerable moments of my life. The parts I tried to hide from the world because I was ashamed, not realizing the testimonies that came from these moments have saved other families.

It's about who you're called to reach because of your healing.

You get free so you can lead.

You surrender so God can stretch your story across generations.

There's a nation waiting on your *yes*.

You're not too late.
You're not too old.
You're not disqualified
You're not too broken.

If you're still breathing, you're still called.

The very fact that you've survived what tried to bury you is evidence that your impact is necessary.

And no, you won't have all the answers.

You may not have all the funding, the support, the connections, or the clarity.

You may be leading with a trembling hand and a tight throat. Let me remind you, faith doesn't always feel like confidence. Sometimes, it feels like fear and you move forward anyway. For every little girl waiting to know she can be healed. For every woman wondering if she can make it out of her abusive marriage. For every person waiting on your assignment so they too can be set free.

There's a nation of women, children, people waiting on you.

This is where purpose goes global.

Not because you have it all figured out.
Not because you feel "ready."

Obedience doesn't require perfection; it just requires your yes.

You don't have to be the loudest voice in the room.
You don't need a title, a following, or a mic.

Leadership in the Kingdom doesn't require a title. It looks like showing up when it's inconvenient, loving people who don't love you back, and pouring out even when your cup is cracked.

Impact doesn't start when you arrive, it begins the moment you move.

So move.
Scared.
Underfunded.
Unseen.
Move anyway.

Because the moment you do, you give permission for every woman watching to do the same. This is much bigger than you Sis.

Recently, God showed me the ripple effect of obedience, and I couldn't hardly swallow afterwards. There was a lump in my throat so big and full of air. I didn't have the capacity to process that I am purpose, purpose is unfolding even before this book is finished.

I wear many hats and made the decision about a year ago to hire a Virtual Assistant from the Philippines to help me bring my vision to life. We started out a little shaky because I wasn't prepared for her. I knew I needed help, but I didn't have the time to train or prepare tasks for her. So I took a step back, prayed about my approach, had a conversation with her and she's been sooo amazing since. She recently sent me a picture of a church she and her husband are building in the Philippines. I thought it was business, but God said, "No, it's Kingdom." Her compensation now helps her family build a *church* in a country I've never stepped foot in.

It's because of my obedience in saying "Yes" to His will, to His purpose for my life that I had to hire her to do the work (completely a divine appointment). Your yes impacts nations, sis. It's so much bigger than you. I really pray you see that.

Let me remind you of the woman who anointed Jesus' feet with oil from the alabaster box. This powerful, unnamed woman known only as "a sinful woman" in Luke 7:36–50. And sis...her story is *impactful*. No, she's not Esther. No, she's not Mary. Her yes was raw, public, messy, and unforgettable.

She wasn't a queen.
She didn't come from wealth.
She didn't have a title, she didn't have a microphone, or a platform.
She had a past and her *Yes*.

She showed up at the Pharisee's house where she didn't even have an invitation.

The Pharisee had invited Jesus to come and eat because he was curious about him, his ways and his teachings. This was around a year or so before the crucifixion, so this was the first of three accounts with a woman with oil anointing Jesus.

Jesus is eating, and talking with the men and this woman (known as a prostitute), this woman - brave, broken, and bold, walked in carrying her most valuable possession: an alabaster jar filled with costly perfume and broke it. Standing behind him, she washed Jesus' feet with her tears, dried them with her hair and then anointed his feet with oil.

She didn't wait for permission.

She broke the jar that she's probably been storing up for years, symbolizing it could never be resealed and poured it all out. The prostitute was purpose. Listen, I don't think you understand. The Pharisee had ill intent when he invited Jesus in, he didn't properly greet Jesus, he didn't offer for Jesus to clean up before eating which was a part of their custom. Yet a prostitute, full of sin (someone the modern day church would silence and cast away or keep in the back closet for their own lustful desires), understood that she needed to yield her life to this "Yes moment." Because she knew it wasn't customary for the women to approach or bother the men while eating or while in discussion she stood behind him. Her intent wasn't to be seen. Her intent was to be yielded.

In biblical times, the perfume was said to be worth about 300 denarii, which was approximately a full year's wages for a laborer.

If we translate that to modern U.S. standards, using the 2024 U.S. median income, her jar was worth between $55,000–$65,000 today.

She didn't give Jesus leftovers. She gave Jesus her best Yes in the moment. She didn't offer what was convenient or budget-friendly.

She gave Him everything she had, her best, her future, her value, her identity and poured it all out at His feet. That "yes moment" is when purpose was fulfilled for Jesus to teach about forgiveness and love and for every man at the table to see He was different. He was THE Messiah. Jesus knew she was a prostitute, he knew she was a sinner, he knew she was unclean and He still allowed her to worship him and then forgave her and saved her. Sis, can you imagine pouring out $60,000 at the feet of Jesus?

No hesitation. No receipt. No refund.

She didn't keep any for herself.

Her "yes moment" was worship.

And her surrender made the room uncomfortable.

While religious men whispered, Jesus watched.
While others judged, Jesus honored her.

And this story has impacted nations for generations. Her "yes moment" was so much bigger than her. Not because of her sin. Not because of her inadequacy. Not because of what she lacked. Not because of her resume.

But because of her pour.
Because of her yes.
She poured it all out.
She wept.

To have enough tears to wash Jesus' feet while standing behind him meant she was weeping. She didn't care about what would happen to her afterwards, she didn't care about being judged by the men.

She worshiped.

Her obedience wasn't polished. It was poured out.

She didn't wait until she was "healed."
She didn't wait until she felt worthy.
She didn't wait for an apology from someone else.
She gave Him what she had, as she was.
And her pour changed the room.

You don't have to wait until you're healed to pour.

You don't have to wait until it's perfect to move.

God is asking for your yes, not your perfection.

Because when you pour, chains break.
When you pour, hearts heal.
When you pour, nations shift.

Sis, you are the assignment.

And your yes, that trembling, surrendered, mustard-seed yes, carries *world-changing oil.*

My Life Poured Out

Affirmations

I am the only me.
I was created with intention,
Designed by God's own hands.
There is no one else like me.
My presence carries weight, my voice carries power, and my uniqueness is my ministry.
I see purpose in all things.
I am not stuck, I'm being shaped.
Even when I don't understand, I trust God's plan.
Every moment in my life has meaning.
God wastes nothing, and I'm living proof.
I was born to impact nations.
I was created for more than survival.
I carry impact in my obedience.
I don't have to be perfect to be powerful.
My purpose will outlive me.
I am making a generational difference by simply showing up.
I say yes, even when I'm afraid because my yes carries oil.

Midwife Moment

Now it's your turn to push, to breathe, to birth something from within.

1. Own what makes you different. What do people compliment you on that you've brushed off or minimized? Write them down. That's evidence of your impact. What have you been told is "too much" about you? Ask God to show you how that very thing might be your assignment in disguise.

2. Where have you been shrinking or holding back out of fear of judgment or comparison? Name the space. Then write how you would show up if you fully believed you were enough.

3. Unlock Purpose in Your Process.
   - What's one season of your life that felt random or painful, but looking back, shaped you? Write what you learned or how you grew.
   - What current situation feels pointless or frustrating? Ask God: "Show me the purpose in this." Journal what He speaks.
   - What areas of your life have you dismissed as "not spiritual enough" that might actually be part of your calling? Parenting? Creativity? Administration? Empathy? Look again.

4. Move in Purpose Anyway.
   - What's one thing God has been asking you to do that you've delayed out of fear or perfectionism? Write it down. Speak it aloud. Declare your yes.
   - Who will benefit from your obedience? List the names of people—family, clients, future generations—who are waiting on your story, your voice, your courage.
   - What's your next faithful step? Not the 5-year plan, just the next right one. Write it down and commit to it this week.

My Life Poured Out

Midwife Moment

Declare this aloud:
"I was made for this. What I carry is rare. Purpose is not far, it's here. God will meet me in my movement. My yes is enough. My story is sacred. My obedience changes nations."

Final Invitation to Purpose

> " Purpose isn't something you find someday, it's something you uncover in everything. "

- Temeka Thompson

Chapter 6

Disclaimer:
If you skipped a chapter, you might want to go back and read it before you accept my final invitation.

From one woman to another.

Sis...you did the dang oh thang.

You made it.
You cried.
You paused.
You laughed.
You journaled.
You wrestled with some hard truths.

And maybe just maybe you started seeing yourself a little differently. I'm praying you did.

Not as the woman who's too late.
Not as the woman who's too broken.
Not as the woman who's too much or not enough.

But as the woman God knew you'd become when you finally decided to say yes.

Now here's the invitation, **don't stop here.**

This isn't the end of a book.
It's the beginning of a movement.

You were never created to simply read about purpose. You were created to **live it, be it.** To walk in it.

To raise daughters, build businesses, speak truth, and shift atmospheres with it.

To unlock healing in places where silence once lived.

To create impact in places that once held you bound.

You may still be scared.
That's okay, I promise.

You may still feel unqualified.
That's okay too, I promise.

But remember what I've been saying all this time, ***Purpose moves in obedience, not perfection.***

So I want to challenge you, with love and with urgency

Go do the thing.
Send the email.
Start the blog.
Forgive the person (or people).
Launch the ministry.
Apply for the job.
Write the book.
Travel the world.
Start that non-profit.
Book the therapy.
Say yes to healing.
Say yes to you.
Say yes to God.

Because nations are waiting.
And you're no longer hidden.
You're seen.
You're called.
You're chosen.
You're ready.

Not perfect, but ready.
Not fearless but willing.

Not empty but filled with enough to take the next step. You don't have to do it all. You just have to do your part.

And I promise you, if you pour out what's in you, God will do the rest.

So here's my final question, will you let your life be poured out?

This isn't the end and I'm not leaving you Sis. If you'd like to stay connected, scan the QR code so we can continue to grow together and move in purpose together.

ABOUT THE AUTHOR

Temeka Thompson is known as The Midwife of Purpose, helping women of faith come out of hiding, find their identity, and boldly walk in their divine calling. A powerhouse in personal development, she is also the Co-Founder of Marriage Takeover® and the visionary behind Daughter Arise ™.

A certified life coach, dynamic speaker, and 9/11 Pentagon survivor, Temeka combines fierce wisdom, lived experience, and radical faith to inspire transformation from the inside out. Whether she's coaching women, mentoring couples, or leading real estate deals across the DMV, her mission remains the same: to help people unlock their next—with obedience, not perfection. Heal Her. Honor Her. Serve Her.

To learn more, connect with her at:
www.temekathompson.com
IG | FB | Tiktok @ iamtemekathompson
IG | FB | Tiktok @ marriagetakeover
Podcast | YouTube @ UnlockHerNext

OTHER BOOKS BY THE AUTHOR

Know your role in your Marriage

Co-authored with Eric Thompson Sr. This Amazon Best-seller will open your eyes to how the husband and the wife abuse their authority and shine light on how important it is to be in God's alignment and fully understand your role in your marriage.

Your Voice Matters

This international best-seller compilation of written offerings is a 100% expression of each contributing author. Each work is published as it was received--unedited, unfiltered, raw-- pure from their hearts and lives. Stirred by the protests and riots of 2020, these authors had something they wanted to share with the World. Their voices matter. Please, listen with an open heart and mind. Just listen.

For more information about the author and her works, visit www.temekathompson.com

ACKNOWLEDGMENTS

Hands down, I couldn't have done this without you God. Without the Holy Spirit guiding me. Without Your healing, Your deliverance, You saving me, You loving me, You seeing me, You guiding me, and Your invitation into real relationship with You. Even up until the very last moments of finishing this book, You kept reminding me to prophesy to the situations, to speak to the distractions that kept rising up and to declare Psalms 91 over my life. I'm so grateful that you love me so much. Thank you for never leaving me nor forsaking me. I'm ten toes down with you any day of the week. To the One who carried the weight when I didn't know how to breathe under it, thank You for meeting me in the places I tried to hide from myself. Thank You for trading my fear for boldness, my shame for identity, my silence for a voice. You are the reason these pages exist.

To my husband, Eric. My rock, my steady place. Thank you for holding space for the version of me that was healing while cheering for the version of me that was becoming and now birthing. I'm glad we stuck through the worst parts of our marriage and learned to heal and love each other more, the fruit is so much better on this side - LOL. Thank you for the late nights (there were many - LOL), and the laughs that had me almost peeing on myself. Thank you for holding me in the moments where I wanted to cry but too prideful and afraid to take my cape off. Thank you for the prayers and for always speaking into my life. Thank you for the protection, covering and leadership. Thank you for loving me so well.

ACKNOWLEDGMENTS

Thank you for the unwavering belief in what God is doing through me. Thank you for always believing in me and being my #1 fan. And thank you for always giving me a soft place to land. 28+ years and I wouldn't want to do it with anyone else. I'm so in love with you .

To my babies: Ej and Aaliyah. Thank you for giving me purpose beyond my own reflection. I've learned so much from being your mother. Thank you for loving me through my wounds and scars as I healed throughout your lives. Aaliyah, thank you for your help with the promo videos and being patient with deadlines. I'm sure I got on your nerves with video demands, and you always pulled through for mommy. And for those hugs when I felt stretched thin. You're amazing at what you do, I can't wait to watch your movies on the big screen, thank you my love. Ej, you got the most unhealed version of me and you turned out to be my greatest lesson in life. I'm so proud of the young man you've become. I can't wait to see the fruits of your labor with the business your building and the legacy you're creating. I'm so proud of you both and love you so much. Thank you for reminding me that legacy starts at home.

ACKNOWLEDGMENTS

I wouldn't exist without you and there are many traces of you both that shine bright for the world to see. There isn't a day that goes by that I wish you were right here with me, taking this all in, laughing with me, watching the kids grow up, going shopping. I know you're proud. I know you're watching over us and I'm so grateful for the life you poured into me. Thank you for being such a great example of being a woman, full of wisdom with a pure and kind heart. Mom, I am because of you. There aren't words that can express how much I miss you and love you.

Daddy, there is no me without you. Time is something we can never get back, but I'm so grateful for God redeeming the time for us. Thank you for allowing me to heal. Thank you for listening, thank you for growing with me. Thank you for your wisdom, thank you for your guidance. Thank you for walking with me through this forgiveness journey, I can't imagine that it was easy all the time - LOL (I do have Kyler blood running through my veins). Thank you so much for taking this journey with me. Thank you for loving me and my family so well. I thank God for you and I love you so much Daddy.

To my instant wardrobe committee, confidant, shoulder to cry on and THE BEST sister in the entire universe. Sis, I finally did it!! Thank you for always being the leveling ground (you remind me so much of momma and her wisdom). Thank you for always making sense of me and helping me to see the calm in my chaos. And thank you for believing in me and praying for me. I'm so proud of you and I know momma is as well. I can't wait to bump your music in my car and my gym workouts...I love you so much!

ACKNOWLEDGMENTS

To my family, every person whose story is interwoven through mine. Thank you for the lessons, the love, the stretching, the breaking, and the rebuilding. Thank you for the moments that shaped me and the moments that saved me. Derrick and Kelli the gym passes to keep me on track (thank you), your support by purchasing a book or sharing it with others. Your prayers. Your encouragement. The joys and laughs of just being around family. And the phone calls and text messages. The quarterly brunches that have become my lifeline. I honor and love each and every one of you. Every aunt, uncle, cousin, niece and nephew, my in-love (law) family. I truly honor the journey. And to the great giants that transitioned during the writing of this book (Uncle Roosevelt, Gramps, Auntie Vera, Auntie Gloria, Auntie Mary), know that your legacy continues. I miss and love you so much.

Worship and Therapy saved my life along with a few amazing coaches and doctors. To my Therapists that walked alongside me as I healed (I went through a few - LOL) - I truly thank God for each of you. To my Mindset Coach Jamal. God knew I needed you in my life and you were so worth the wait. What an amazing gift you are to this world, thank you for your Yes to your calling. I thank God for you often. Thank you for helping me to experience God differently and to step into my identity. And thank you for believing in me. Coach Keith, I locked in and we did it!!! I thank God for you dude. I don't think I could've gotten stronger and dropped this weight without Cardio Combat and the personal training. Thank you for not giving up on me. Thank you for hearing God as it relates to my life. Thank you for the wisdom and helping me to stay on track. I'm stronger, healthier and more confident than I've been since graduating from basic training. Thank you. Shift Dr. Joy, Honey!!! Can you believe we made it? I know you can, thank you so much for seeing what God is doing in me and for meeting me in South Carolina and nurturing all that God was doing in me. I appreciate you, I appreciate what God is doing in you. I love you so much Sis and thank God for you. Thank you for believing in me. Tunisicia O, you will always be my Forgiveness Coach! Thank you for seeing me. It was your workshop that shifted my forgiveness journey in motion. Thank you for your transparency and the gift of you. You are so amazing at what you do. Wyevetra, thank you beautiful for always being such a great inspiration to my life and an awesome example and mentor when it comes to real estate, family and business. And for showing me it's okay for me to trust and lean in again. I love you and appreciate you.

To the best doctors in the DMV, thank you so much for taking this journey with me and being patient with me. Dr. Williams, I know it isn't always easy (especially when it comes to my blood pressure - LOL). Dr. Baxi, you and your team were instrumental in me stepping into purpose after the hysterectomy and the tumor removal. Thank you for being a part of the village that saved my life.

Zo, can you believe we're here? It was literally 20 years ago and you were designing my CD cover. Thank you for always being solid on the designs. I appreciate you so much.

ACKNOWLEDGMENTS

Arielle, thank you for always having my face beat. It's been 11+ years. The conversations we've had...Can't wait for you to release your book and stop playing around - LOL.

Mrs. Donna, time flies when you're connected with amazing people. Thank you for always being so solid for my family. I love you, I honor you and thank you so much for the gift of you.

Thank you to each and every one of my friends. The laughs, the tears, the growth. Thank you for loving me flaws and all. I love you.

To my family, those I was blessed to meet and love because I chose forgiveness. What was once distant became sacred when I released the weight of pain and opened my heart. My yes to forgiveness unlocked doors I had long prayed for, allowing me to know, embrace, and belong to the family I had always yearned for. You are a living reminder that healing restores more than hearts, it restores connection. My uncles in Detroit, I love you guys so much. Thank you all so much for loving me and my family and never making us feel like outsiders. The long, amazing conversations, phone calls, check-ins. Thank you. My aunts in Georgia and Florida, I love you and appreciate you. The visits, the texts, sharing trip experiences, always taking care of and thinking about baby girl, I love it all. If I start naming everyone, I'm gonna be in trouble, but thank you so much for the phone calls, the text messages, the nudges, the laughs - OMG and the raw transparency.

ACKNOWLEDGMENTS

To the cousins, I've met over the years, the rich history and legacy I've learned so much about, thank you for love. And to know, we're direct descendants of Rosewood, who would've thought? Rich history and legacy on both sides of the family. Ford's & Kyler's are built tough baby! I love you all so much!

I'm so grateful I chose the gift of forgiveness.

Who would've ever thought my Yes would give me a footprint in the Philippines? When I tell you, there's a nation of women waiting on your yes. Jesa, thank you for honoring God with your work. Thank you for leading with God first in your life. And thank you for being such an absolute blessing to my life. Keeping me together while I was running two businesses, having a life and working full-time. Thank you for keeping me together - LOL!! Thank you for always being available when I needed you most. Thank you for your prayers. Thank you for hanging in there with me when I was trying to figure everything out. I appreciate you so much and thank God for you every single day. Thank you for taking things off of my plate and making room so I could step into purpose.

To my Marriage Takeover® family, thank you for showing up, growing, stretching, healing, and transforming. Through Wife's Lounge and coaching sessions, you helped me step into the Midwife of Purpose.

ACKNOWLEDGMENTS

To Byrd's World Publishing and Sisters (Re) Sisters, thank you for helping me honor this story with excellence. Your Feedback sessions, developmental editing and final proofreading helped polish the raw sincerity of these pages without dimming the authenticity of my voice. Heather, you are the BEST to do it in the publishing world. Your genius in this space is unmatched when it comes to ensuring the story comes alive. Thank you! Jasminum, baby, your word smithing, is a treasure. Thank you for the late hours and meeting the deadlines and answering all of my silly questions. I appreciate you so much beautiful. I'm so grateful to you all. I know Regina is smiling down on us.

To my Purpose Pushers, my launch team thank you for believing in this book before the world ever saw it. Thank you for reading it, thank you for your testimonials, your prayers, your excitement, your prophetic confirmations, and the way you carried this assignment with me. I appreciate and love you ladies.

To every woman who sent feedback, who cried through a chapter, who said, "Temeka, you made a place for me," thank you. I wrote these pages for you, but your responses told me God wrote them for us.

To the women reading this book, you are my assignment and the reason I write. Thank you for being brave enough to pick this up. It's one thing to pick up the book, it's another thing to finish it, so thank you for being brave enough to finish it.

ACKNOWLEDGMENTS

Thank you for being willing to confront what hurt you, silenced you, or convinced you that God made a mistake when He called you. You are the reason this book breathes. You are the reason these words have weight. I pray you step into the fullness of who you are with courage and clarity.

To the girl I used to be, thank you for surviving long enough for me to find you. Thank you for holding on. Thank you for dreaming even when you were discouraged. Thank you for choosing obedience even when perfection felt safer. Look at us now.

And to the woman I'm becoming, thank you for saying yes. Over and over again.

www.ingramcontent.com/pod-product-compliance
Ingram Content Group UK Ltd.
Pitfield, Milton Keynes, MK11 3LW, UK
UKHW041638190726
13854UKWH00006B/2576